THE GREEK TRAGEDY
IN NEW TRANSLATIONS

GENERAL EDITOR   William Arrowsmith

AESCHYLUS: **Seven Against Thebes**

AESCHYLUS

Seven Against Thebes

Translated by
ANTHONY HECHT

and
HELEN H. BACON

OXFORD UNIVERSITY PRESS
New York and London
1973

Printed in the United States of America

To Frank E. Brown

EDITOR'S FOREWORD

The Greek Tragedy in New Translations is based on the conviction that poets like Aeschylus, Sophocles, and Euripides can only be properly rendered by translators who are themselves poets. Scholars may, it is true, produce useful and perceptive versions. But our most urgent present need is for a *re-creation* of these plays—as though they had been written, freshly and greatly, by masters fully at home in the English of our own times. Unless the translator is a poet, his original is likely to reach us in crippled form: deprived of the power and pertinence it must have if it is to speak to us of what is permanent in the Greek. But poetry is not enough; the translator must obviously know what he is doing, or he is bound to do it badly. Clearly, few contemporary poets possess enough Greek to undertake the complex and formidable task of transplanting a Greek play without also "colonializing" it or stripping it of its deep cultural difference, its remoteness from us. And that means depriving the play of that crucial *otherness* of Greek experience—a quality no less valuable to us than its closeness. Collaboration between scholar and poet is therefore the essential operating principle of the series. In fortunate cases scholar and poet co-exist; elsewhere we have teamed able poets and scholars in an effort to supply, through affinity and intimate collaboration, the necessary combination of skills.

An effort has been made to provide the general reader or student with first-rate critical introductions, clear expositions of translators' principles, commentary on difficult passages, ample stage directions, and glossaries of mythical and geographical terms encountered in the plays. Our purpose throughout has been to make the reading of the plays as vivid as possible. But our poets have constantly tried to remember that they were translating *plays*—plays meant to be produced, in language that actors could speak, naturally and with dignity. The poetry aims at being *dramatic* poetry and realizing itself in words and actions that are both speakable and playable.

Finally, the reader should perhaps be aware that no pains have been spared in order that the "minor" plays should be translated as carefully and brilliantly as the acknowledged masterpieces. For the Greek Tragedy in New Translations aims to be, in the fullest sense, *new*. If we need vigorous new poetic versions, we also need to see the plays with fresh eyes, to reassess the plays *for ourselves*, in terms of our own needs. This means translations that liberate us from the canons of an earlier age because the translators have recognized, and discovered, in often neglected works, the perceptions and wisdom that make these works ours and necessary to us.

A NOTE ON THE SERIES FORMAT

If only for the illusion of coherence, a series of thirty-three Greek plays requires a consistent format. Different translators, each with his individual voice, cannot possibly develop the sense of a single coherent style for each of the three tragedians; nor even the illusion that, despite their differences, the tragedians share a common set of conventions and a generic, or period, style. But they can at least share a common approach to orthography and a common vocabulary of conventions.

1. *Spelling of Greek Names*

Adherence to the old convention whereby Greek names were first Latinized before being housed in English is gradually disappearing. We are now clearly moving away from Latinization and toward precise transliteration. The break with tradition may be regrettable, but there is much to be said for hearing and seeing Greek names as though they were both Greek and *new*, instead of Roman or neoclassical importations. We cannot of course see them as wholly new. For better or worse certain names and myths are too deeply rooted in our literature and thought to be dislodged. To speak of "Helene" and "Hekabe" would be no less pedantic and absurd than to write "Aischylos' " or "Platon" or "Thoukydides." There are of course borderline cases. "Jocasta" (as opposed to "Iokaste") is not a major mythical figure in her own right; her familiarity in her Latin form is a function of the fame of Sophocles' play as the tragedy *par excellence*. And as tourists we go to Delphi, not Delphoi. The precisely transliterated form may be pedantically "right," but the pedantry goes against the grain of cultural habit and actual usage.

As a general rule, we have therefore adopted a "mixed" orthography according to the principles suggested above. When a name has been firmly housed in English (admittedly the question of domestication is often moot), the traditional spelling has been kept. Otherwise names have been transliterated. Throughout the series the *-os* termination of masculine names has been adopted, and Greek diphthongs (as in Iphigeneia) have normally been retained. We cannot expect complete agreement from readers (or from translators, for that matter) about borderline cases. But we want at least to make the operative principle clear: to walk a narrow line between orthographical extremes in the hope of keeping what should not, if possible, be lost; and refreshing, in however tenuous a way, the specific sound and name-boundedness of Greek experience.

2. Stage directions

The ancient manuscripts of the Greek plays do not supply stage directions (though the ancient commentators often provide information relevant to staging, delivery, "blocking," etc.). Hence stage directions must be inferred from words and situations and our knowledge of Greek theatrical conventions. At best this is a ticklish and uncertain procedure. But it is surely preferable that good stage directions should be provided by the translator than that the reader should be left to his own devices in visualizing action, gesture, and spectacle. Obviously the directions supplied should be both spare and defensible. Ancient tragedy was austere and "distanced" by means of masks, which means that the reader must not expect the detailed intimacy ("He shrugs and turns wearily away," "She speaks with deliberate slowness, as though to emphasize the point," etc.) which characterizes stage directions in modern naturalistic drama. Because Greek drama is highly rhetorical and stylized, the translator knows that his words must do the real work of inflection and nuance. Therefore every effort has been made to supply the visual and tonal sense required by a given scene and the reader's (or actor's) putative unfamiliarity with the ancient conventions.

3. Numbering of lines.

For the convenience of the reader who may wish to check the English against the Greek text or vice versa, the lines have been numbered according to both the Greek text and the translation. The lines of the English translation have been numbered in multiples of ten, and these numbers have been set in the right-hand margin. The (inclusive) Greek numeration will be found bracketed at the top of the page. The reader will doubtless note that in many plays the English lines outnumber the Greek, but he should not therefore conclude that the translator has been unduly prolix. In most cases the reason is simply that the translator has adopted the free-flowing norms of modern Anglo-American prosody, with its brief, breath- and emphasis-determined lines, and its habit of indicating cadence and caesuras by line length and setting rather than by conventional punctuation. Other translators have preferred four-beat or five-beat lines, and in these cases Greek and English numerations will tend to converge.

4. Notes and Glossary

In addition to the Introduction, each play has been supplemented by Notes (identified by the line numbers of the translation) and a Glossary. The Notes are meant to supply information which the translators deem important to the interpretation of a passage; they also afford the translator an opportunity to justify what he has done. The Glossary is intended to spare the reader the trouble of going elsewhere to look up mythical or geographical terms. The entries are not meant to be comprehensive; when a fuller explanation is needed, it will be found in the Notes.

ABOUT THE TRANSLATION

This translation of Aeschylus' *Seven Against Thebes* is the result of close and sympathetic collaboration between a distinguished poet and a classical scholar of unusual critical insight and judgment.

Anthony Hecht has received the Pulitzer Prize for Poetry (1968) and the Loine Award of the National Institute of Arts and Letters. His first book, *A Summoning of Stones* (1954), was followed by *The Seven Deadly Sins* (1958), *A Bestiary* (1960), and *The Hard Hours* (1967). He has taught at Bard College and is now professor of English at the University of Rochester. Among his honors are a fellowship in poetry from The American Academy in Rome, a fellowship from the Ford Foundation, and Brandeis University's Creative Arts Award.

Hecht's collaborator, Helen H. Bacon, is presently professor of Classics at Barnard College. Educated at Bryn Mawr and Berkeley, she has been scholar-in-residence at The American Academy in Rome, a Fulbright fellow, and a fellow of The American School of Classical Studies in Athens. In addition to numerous pieces in classical journals, she is the author of *Barbarians in Greek Tragedy* (1961) and a forthcoming critical monograph of *Seven Against Thebes*.

The special distinction of this new poetic version of *Seven Against Thebes* is, I believe, that it redeems a play commonly regarded as "minor" and shows, in realized dramatic poetry enabled by unusual critical perception, the full justice of its claim to be a major work of a great dramatist. In this respect the translation should be viewed, not as a rediscovery, but as a genuine discovery. Although highly esteemed in antiquity, *Seven Against Thebes* has become the Cinderella of the Aeschylean corpus, neglected or dismissed because it was thought to be textually corrupt or incoherent and "episodic"— that is, lacking in the unity so tanglible in the *Agamemnon* and *Prometheus* or even *The Persians*. Even its choral poetry has found few admirers because it is so deeply knitted into the internal dynamics of the action and texture, and therefore offers few "lyrical" opportunities or conveniently detachable odes. What Hecht and Bacon have restored is not only a true and powerful tragedy (in place of the flawed episodic set-piece of the handbooks), but the feeling and thought on which that tragedy rests: the dramatist's Eleusinian sense of life, the patterns of human destiny grounded in the archaic poetry of the Greek earth. For the first time, I believe, Professor Bacon demonstrates that the "heraldic" and "episodic" qualities of the play are integrated in a comprehensive thematic design; and her demonstration is transformed into radiant poetic and dramatic action by Hecht. The result is a play which, far from being without unity and power, is clearly a single, seamless dramatic tissue, fully tragic, and as playable as it is readable.

Lincoln, Vermont   William Arrowsmith

CONTENTS

SEVEN AGAINST THEBES

INTRODUCTION

I

With some important exceptions, scholars and translators, from the nineteenth century onwards, have been virtually at one in their indifference to *Seven Against Thebes*; an indifference which has been deflected from time to time only into overt hostility and contempt. The play has been accused of being static, undramatic, ritualistic, guilty of an interpolated and debased text, archaic, and, in a word, boring. The present translators find themselves in profound disagreement with such assessments, and cherish a slight hope that the translation offered here—which is also an interpretation, as any translation must be—will help restore to the play some of the dramatic and literary interest it deserves to have even for those with no knowledge of Greek.

This translation has aimed at literal accuracy insofar as that was possible within the limitations of our own imaginations and understanding; our English text departs from the original mainly through that sort of extrapolation we have thought useful to a modern audience not likely to be acquainted with all the minor Greek deities, for example, or with their ritual attributes. Thus, where Phobos alone will do in the original, here he is identified as the god of fear. This kind of expansion, as well as complete independence from the Greek of the English lineation, has made our text some three hundred lines longer than the original. But we are confident—as confident as our scruples and a certain fitting modesty will allow us to be—that in this we have not violated the tone or dramatic intention of the play. A scholarly defense of such liberties as we may be thought to have taken will appear, as it ought to, elsewhere.

Still, it must be admitted that even to the most sympathetic of readers *Seven Against Thebes* suffers under a special handicap. It is the last play of a trilogy of which the first two plays have been lost. It is, of course, impossible accurately to reconstruct the enormous dramatic and linguistic forces that must have been contrived and set in motion to culminate in this play; but one may perhaps guess at the magnitude of the loss if one were to think of the *Oresteia* as surviving only in the text of the *Eumenides*. We do know the names of the first two plays of this trilogy: *Laios* and *Oedipus*. And what we know of the ancient legends and sagas of the Curse of the house of Laios, of the traditional lore concerning the founding of Thebes by Kadmos, and of the subsequent history of the city, may provide us with some of the background with which Aeschylus approached this final drama in the series.

II

Like the "history" of the Trojan War, Theban "history" was preserved in epic poems, now lost, but almost as familiar to fifth-century Athenians as the *Iliad* and *Odyssey*. Aeschylus could count on his audience knowing not only his specific shaping of the stories of Laios and Oedipus in the two earlier plays, but also the broad outlines of the whole story of Thebes as preserved in the poetic tradition. It is a story of violence and wrath from beginning to end.

Kadmos, the founder of the city and the royal house, came from Tyre seeking his sister Europa. He killed a dragon that guarded a spring at what would become the site of Thebes and, at Athena's direction, sowed the dragon's teeth in earth. The teeth sprouted as a crop of armed men who, when Kadmos pelted them with stones, began to murder each other. The five survivors of this fratricidal battle, the so-called "sown men" (Spartoi), were the ancestors of the people of Thebes. The lost epics went on to tell the stories of Laios and his descendants, but did not end, as the trilogy does, with the defeat of the Argive army, the death in battle of the army's leaders, and the fratricide of the sons of Oedipus. They pursued a narrative that took up the story again ten years later when, just before the Trojan War, the sons of the leaders of the Argives returned for their revenge at the head of another Argive army, and completely destroyed Thebes. This sack of Thebes by the Epigonoi, as the sons of the seven Argive captains were called, was one of the most firmly fixed elements of the tradition: among the famous cities of Greece, only Thebes is missing from the catalogue of the ships in the *Iliad*. Aeschylus' audience could not fail to associate the many hints of future disaster for Thebes appearing throughout this play with the total destruction of that city by the sons of the "Seven."

The principal mythological figures of *Seven Against Thebes*, Ares, the Fury, the Curse (also referred to in the plural as Curses, perhaps suggesting the separate words of the imprecation), Dike, and Apollo, interact in a context taken for granted by Aeschylus' audience, but which for us perhaps requires some explanation. Ares, the Fury, and the personified Curse of the house of Laios (the Curse of which Laios and Oedipus were the victims and which in turn Oedipus laid upon his two sons) represent the forces which are let loose when Dike, the personification of the fundamental principle of right and order, is violated. The trilogy dramatized a chain of outrages (outlined in this play in the third choral song, 908-1009,[1] the Fury chorus) starting with Laios' defiance of Apollo's word—which said that if Laios refrained from begetting offspring the city would be safe. The traditional reason for this prohibition was that Laios had kidnaped, violated, and murdered the little son of his host and friend, Pelops. For this violation of the sacred tie of hospitality, childlessness was a fitting punishment. Like the banquet of Thyestes in *Agamemnon*, this, or a similar outrage, was probably the crime behind the crimes in *Laios*. To these acts of violence, Laios added the attempt to destroy his own son, Oedipus, the child of forbidden intercourse. And violence begets violence. Oedipus killed his father and married his mother; his sons, by an act of outrage against him (we do not know which of several versions of their crime Aeschylus used in *Oedipus*), provoked their father's Curse, and they then attempted to take possession of their mother city by violence (Aeschylus in the lament (1118-29) makes plain that Eteokles too has used force on Thebes) and ended by murdering each other. Dike represents the sanctity of the basic relationships between god and man, host and guest, parent and child, brother and brother, relationships which Laios and his descendants defied. When these are violated Dike is violated.

The Fury, wrath (her Greek name Erinys is derived from *eris*, wrath or strife), and Ares, violence and hostility, are the instruments with which Zeus comes to the defense of Dike, but they are in turn the cause of new outrages in an apparently endless sequence. The Curse is another expression of the same psychological fact. It is the

1. Unless otherwise indicated, line references throughout are to our English version.

prayer of a victim, which is implemented by Ares and the Fury in their capacity as enforcers of Dike. Where this complex of forces occurs Delphic Apollo will always be found as well, in his role as restorer of harmony and health, the purifier from all kinds of contagion. Only when the miasma of violated Dike has been cleansed away does the Fury cease raging and become the gentle cherisher that she is at the end of the *Oresteia*. Though in *Seven Against Thebes* she appears only as a destroyer, it should not be forgotten that she destroys in defense of the helpless and in order that life and the social order that sustains life shall be cherished. Her contradictoriness is the contradictoriness of woman—the tender mother ready to kill in defense of those she cherishes. Several images and figures in this play express this enigmatic quality of the female—the moon, Hekate, Artemis, the land of Thebes, the Sphinx (notes to 473 and 661).

An Athenian audience would also have recognized the parallels in *Seven Against Thebes* with their own recent history, and responded to them with a special set of feelings and values. The return of an exiled ruler to claim his rights with the support of a foreign army, a not infrequent occurrence in Greece, was regarded with the same kind of religious horror as was felt toward attacks on parents. *Seven Against Thebes* was produced in 467 B.C. Twenty-three years earlier, in 490 B.C., Hippias, the exiled son of the tyrant, Peisistratos, and himself a former tyrant, landed at Marathon with the Persian army, prepared to be reinstated as ruler of the Athenians. According to Herodotos (VI, 107), whose account is later than our play and could even have been influenced by it, the night before the landing Hippias dreamed that he slept with his mother. At first he interpreted this hopefully, as a sign that he would pass his old age peacefully in Athens. However, when he landed there was another portent. He was seized with a fit of sneezing and coughing, and, being an old man, coughed out one of his teeth, which fell upon his native soil and could not be found again. He then said, "This land is not ours and we will not be able to conquer it. My tooth has my whole share of it." Herodotos adds that this statement was Hippias' interpretation of the dream. In this story, as in *Seven Against Thebes*, the attack on the parent land is equated with incest, and its consequence is that the attacker receives only a token share of his native soil. Hippias received as much Attic earth as his tooth possessed, Eteokles and Polyneices each as much Theban earth as it takes to bury a man. Whether this story of Hippias is older than

Aeschylus' play, or came into being as a result of it, its existence suggests that the Athenians would have understood the play in the light of their own great national crisis. It also suggests that parallels between the crimes of Oedipus and those of his sons would have been more immediately obvious to the Athenians than they are to a modern audience.

III

The action of *Seven Against Thebes* we conceive to be profoundly unified and profoundly dramatic. It unfolds in four stages, of which the Fury is the organizing principle. In the first stage the Fury is set in motion when Eteokles calls on her in conjunction with his father's Curse, to defend the city which is being attacked by one of her own children (96-107). In his prayer Eteokles seems clearly to assume that if any violation against Dike has been or is being committed it is by his brother, Polyneices; he seems to have forgotten or blocked out of his mind the earlier crimes performed jointly with his brother that brought down on both their heads their father's Curse; and seems as well to have forgotten that his exiled brother has as much right as he to be king in Thebes. In the second stage the Fury comes to the defense of Dike by implementing the Curse. She rages unchecked as Eteokles decides to meet his brother in single combat (816-907). In the third stage, Dike is temporarily re-established and the Fury seems to subside. The inheritance is justly divided when the brothers, in death, are apportioned their equal shares of Theban earth. The plays ends with a new outbreak of the Fury as the magistrates of Thebes reopen the conflict by refusing burial to Polyneices —refusing him, that is, his just share of the inheritance—and in so doing once more implicate the city in the fate of the house of Laios, edging Thebes and her entire population one step nearer to their ultimate destruction at the hands of the Epigonoi.

Modern scholars, with a few notable exceptions, regard this last scene, which dramatizes the final stage, as a fourth-century interpolation whose purpose is to bring the play into line with the popular Sophoclean version of the aftermath of the brothers' deaths. They see no justification for introducing a new speaking role in the person of Antigone, who raises what they consider to be a problem new to this play and wholly outside the dramatic unity of its action: the problem of the burial of Polyneices, after the conflict of the brothers has been resolved. Yet the scene is integrated with the entire design of the play; and to an audience familiar with the Theban epics, the second song of the Chorus (362-451), which visualizes the sack of the city, is not an unfulfilled fear but a prophecy of her ultimate fate. And that prophecy is brought nearer to its consummation in this final scene when the city brings upon herself the promise of total annihilation by repeating Eteokles' repudiation of Dike. The scale of the tragedy is enlarged, pity and fear intensified by this fresh outbreak of the Fury. It is not a new problem but a new stage and development of the old problem: how to allay the wrath let loose in Thebes by the chain of outrages stemming from Laios' original violation of Dike. It is a wrath that spreads from the individual members of the house of Laios until it includes, first, the magistrates of Thebes rising up to deny Polyneices his inheritance, and ultimately all the inhabitants of the city that is to be brought to destruction; a wrath that promises a countering wrath, a continued struggle to an exhausted and demolishing end.

IV

The language of *Seven Against Thebes* is markedly concerned with noise, and with two kinds of noise in particular: the noise of battle and the noise of lamentation, that is, of strife and of weeping. At the start of the play, the noise of battle is outside the walls of Thebes, and the noise of lamentation (in the form of the first choral song, 108-212) within. By the time the drama is over, these two noises will come to be identified with the two contending brothers, Eteokles and Polyneices; and not merely because one has been inside and the other outside the walls, but because of their names and their fates, as will appear. Eteokles is more than merely "justifiably angered" by the fears and lamentations of the Chorus: he is enraged and unhinged by them, and proceeds to some quite extraordinary calumnies upon womankind in general. His nominal grounds for wrath are that the Chorus, by their womanly weakness, are undermining manly courage and endangering military morale inside the city. There is a certain plausibility to this, to which, after all, the Chorus acquiesce. But Eteokles' rage seems so extravagant that we might at first suppose that he is himself afraid of losing his nerve. Since, in the event, this does not prove to be the case, there must be some other reason for it. And, indeed, as the drama unfolds, we come to see that this play is not merely the culmination but the terrible re-enactment of the tragedies of Laios and Oedipus, of disobedience, parricide, and incest. And Eteokles' misogyny might be not only an unconscious sense of his inheritance, but a fear that he is doomed to repeat it. He is determined not to. Nevertheless, he does.

As in the case of his father, he is called upon to protect Thebes from what appears to be an outward danger. And, as in his father's case, he seems to undertake this in a manly way. The city of Thebes and its outlying pastures and folds are consistently spoken of in maternal terms, in metaphors of a mother who nurtured, cherished, and brought up her sons, and who must therefore not be violated. The violent desire for exclusive possession of the mother is a tragedy Oedipus unconsciously acted out, becoming blind that he might see what he could not see with his eyes. The violent desire for the exclusive possession of the mother land, the unwillingness of either to be content with a lesser or equal share, drives Oedipus' two sons, who are also his brothers, to murder each other, each one blindly believing justice to be on his side. And each, by murdering his brother, sheds his father's blood. As in the case of Oedipus, a problem is posed, a riddle must be untangled, in order that the city may be saved. For Eteokles this is, in fact, not one riddle but seven. These are the devices on the shields of the seven champions who attack the city.

It may be worth attending to this scene (457-907) in some detail, for it has often been singled out as one of the most tedious blemishes of the play, and it constitutes about a third of the whole. In hearing the report of the Scout and undertaking to construe in terms of magic and numinous power the nature of each of seven successive threats to Thebes, and in proposing a counter-magic for the defense of the city, Eteokles is taking upon himself the role of seer, as once his father did. Yet even before these seven opportunities for divination occur, Eteokles has several times been warned; what he is at pains to conceal from himself is precisely who he is, the nature of his inheritance, and the possibility that he cannot see everything clearly and for what it is. And while the Scout punctiliously addresses him as "most fittingly king of the Kadmeians," the Chorus, with more intimacy and greater point, address him as "son of Oedipus." Moreover, in their high-strung emotional debate with him, they defend their devotion to and utter reliance on the gods by observing that not only are the gods more powerful than men, but that the gods alone can assist humankind when its vision and understanding are obscured. These are implicit warnings against blindness and impiety, and they are augmented by the off-stage but telling presences of two genuine seers and diviners, who are also priests: Teiresias and Amphiaraos. Nevertheless, as commander of the defending troops, Eteokles does not hesitate to assume the role of seer.

There are seven contending champions, and therefore, seven riddles (though there is in addition one great and central riddle, concerning Eteokles' name, which lies at the very heart of the play, and which we will come to later). In general, it may be said that Eteokles conceives these riddles as applying purely to the fate of the contending champions and, by extension, to the fate of Thebes; never does he seem to suppose that the riddles might have any bearing upon his own fate. It may be added that with most of the defending champions he nominates, Eteokles takes pains to advertise the distinction of their genealogies as well as their military prowess and excellence of character. This is, of course, quite in accordance with heroic tradition. But in emphasizing the nativity—the legitimacy, as it were —of these local sons of the mother land, their title by birthright to be her defenders, he appears never to consider that this is a right he must, by the same token, share equally with his own brother. And the fact that two of the defending champions, Hyperbios and Aktor, are themselves brothers, does nothing to remind him of this.

1. The first of the attacking champions is Tydeus. We learn that he abuses and insults a priest of Apollo, Amphiaraos. Yet, while Eteokles does not hesitate to accuse Tydeus of impiety (as indeed he does in the case of every attacker but one—and that one worth noting), neither does he scruple himself to abuse and insult Amphiaraos when later the priest, the true seer, presents himself as the sixth of the champions outside the walls. It is true that Eteokles cannot quite bring himself to accuse so unblemished a man as Amphiaraos of impiety; but the priest is charged with blindness and bad judgment, which Eteokles might do well to consider with respect to himself. And in abusing Amphiaraos, he is imitating the impious enemy, Tydeus. In addition to the dark night (ignorance, inability to see) which is Tydeus' device, the moon, associated with Hekate, goddess of the three ways, might serve to remind Eteokles of the beginning of his father's catastrophe, the curse of the house of Laios, the penalty for blindness. Tydeus' helmet is triple-crested, a part of the riddle to which we will return in due course. Most importantly, Eteokles proclaims that his defending champion, Melanippos, is a blood-relative of Dike, "goddess of all orders, of justice human and divine," and that she will favor him. If Dike is to side with the de-

fending forces, she cannot at the same time side with the attackers, as from the claims of Polyneices it appears she does, unless she is to play some impartial role, and deal with the claims of both sides as being equal.

2. The second of the attackers, Kapaneus, the giant, is an enlargement, a grotesque exaggeration, of the impiety of Tydeus; he defies all the gods, and Zeus in particular. As opposed to Tydeus, whose emblem was darkness, Kapaneus' device is a naked man armed with a flaming torch (which is light and knowledge, the ability to see, to construe the truth), but this light has been perverted into a destructive weapon, intended to reduce the city to ashes (just as the Chorus has feared and prophesied). It might therefore be a warning to Eteokles in his self-assumed office of seer.

3. The third is Eteoklos, whose name is so close to the protagonist's as surely to invite a moment's thought. He is clearly "Eteokles Beyond the Walls," the attacking double of the defender; Eteokles, by this extension, is both outside and inside the city, and therefore it is folly to fear, to observe, to take precautions chiefly against the danger of what is outside. Here is a representation of Eteokles as his own worst enemy, and, pointedly, he has nothing whatever to say about the character of this attacker. Whereas in every other case he is quick to bring accusations of blasphemy, impiety, and folly, here he moves swiftly to name his chosen defender, and makes unusually brisk work of the matter, turning instantly to the next contender.

4. This is Hippomedon, who bears Typhon, the earth god, on his shield. Now, from the very first speech of Eteokles, the earth has been seen as a nourishing parent, child-bearer, kindly provider. But just as the Fury has what seems to be a double nature, or at least two aspects of a single nature, so here is the earth transformed, represented by a monstrous offspring, "breathing fire, black smoke, sister of glittering fire, pouring from his mouth," the universal tomb. This is not unlike the earlier vision of the Chorus.

5. Parthenopaios, "savage-minded" but with a boyish beauty, himself suggests the two aspects of the Fury. And his device, the Sphinx, not only recalls the whole Theban and family saga, but specifically points it toward the problem of knowing who you are. It is declared of Parthenopaios that he reverses his blade "above god and his own eyes," which is to say that he puts violence, military glory, and ambition above piety and knowledge; and it recalls the theme of blindness.

6. The case of Amphiaraos is rich and complicated. He is, first, a

priest of Apollo, the god who is foreteller, knower of what awaits, who long ago warned Laios of what would happen if he begot a child, and who warned the youthful Oedipus of his parricidal and incestuous fate. These facts are all clearly known to the Chorus, and therefore may be supposed to be known to Eteokles as well. As the god's priest, Amphiaraos is not merely a holy man, one who wishes not to seem but in fact to be the best, undeceived by appearances and undeceiving; he also has special access to the wisdom of the god. He clearly denounces the impiety, violence, and violation that Tydeus and Polyneices are about to offer the city, and in the most condemnatory terms; he speaks of this in the highly charged language and metaphor of rape and incest. Eteokles' answer to this riddle is noticeably weak and evasive. Perhaps that is because there is no device for him to perform magic with. But possibly the true piety and self-knowledge of this man has come home to him. In any case, he makes Amphiaraos guilty by association, and, while not doubting the priest's piety—which, incidentally, consists in part in his refusal to attack the city—all but calls him foolish and blind for getting mixed up with wicked men against his better judgment, that is to say, ignorantly. Yet if, as Eteokles himself says, Apollo does not lie, then all the prophecies of disaster which have been accumulating throughout the drama, and which Eteokles has now been given six chances to fathom and to attempt to avert, are obviously pointing to something he does not see, yet knows to be inexorable.

7. At last, the brother, mighty Polyneices (784-815). His claim is plain, violent and sexual.

He declares he will scale and bestride the walls,
proclaimed lord and subjugator of the land.

He makes explicit his equality with Eteokles (which Eteokles has never acknowledged):

he will fight you hand to hand;
and either, in killing you, lie dead beside you,
or else drive you into dishonored exile
just as you forced such banishment on him.

The insistence on "equality" in Polyneices' boast should be noticed. He does not propose, as he might, to kill his brother and take upon himself the kingship; rather he says that either they shall both die, or they shall change places with each other. And just as Eteokles has done, he calls upon the gods of the race of his own land, entreating their support. This exclusive claim to the motherland as a sexual possession is stated at its clearest in Polyneices' device.

A stately woman guides forward a warrior
in full armor who is hammered out in gold.
She says she is Dike—goddess of all orders,
human and divine—
and inscribed there are these words:
"I shall bring this man to his harbor,
and he shall enjoy his father's city,
shall tumble and make free with his house."

The great blow, and the final irony, for Eteokles, is not that his brother should be revealed as a champion, for it was generally known that his brother was among the attacking troops, and no doubt the entire siege has been undertaken at his behest and with an eye to his restoration to the kingship. Clearly, then, he could have been expected to play a major role in the attack. What unhinges Eteokles is in part the claim that Dike is aligned with the forces outside the walls, and with his brother in particular, since he has already assumed that she has allied herself with the defenders. Her impartiality in this, as well perhaps as the discovery that Eteokles is not only inside but outside the walls in the person of Eteoklos, reveal to us at last the true equality of the two brothers in their inheritance, their fate, their shared guilt of origin and of ambition.

But this sense of equality Eteokles is determined to resist to the end, and while he feels he has been mocked and manipulated by fate, he goes to meet his brother in a frenzy of blindness, a man fully armed, turned into iron, himself a weapon. And the Chorus, perhaps recalling the warning that appeared with the very first of the attackers, the triple-crested helmet of Tydeus, proceeds, in the next ode (908-1009), to recall the first of all the warnings to this blind family:

Three times the Lord Apollo
in the midmost Pythian navel,
the prophetic center, spoke:
If Laios were to live
childless, without issue,
then the city would be safe.

And they echo the present storm outside the walls:

Like a plunging and storm-agitated sea,
    disaster drives the wave;
first one wave falls, a second rises up,

a third, three-crested, crashes at the stern
  of the city in angry foam.
  Between our perilous home
  and total jeopardy,
our hull is the mere width of the city walls.

While it is clear enough that, in the first instance, these waves represent the hordes of attacking troops, they have also by this time come to refer to the three destructive and self-destructive generations of the house of Laios, each of which in turn put Thebes in peril, and were themselves the whole cause of her troubles, and, in effect, her attackers.

V

Like Oedipus, whose name means both "knowing foot" and "swollen foot," the sons of Oedipus have names which express their fates. The applicability of Polyneices' name, "full of strife," to his actions as the leader of a foreign army attacking his native city is reasonably clear. Amphiaraos, Eteokles, and finally the Chorus, all brood over it in the section of the play (701-907) that leads up to Eteokles' climactic decision to meet his brother in single combat. The etymologically correct meaning of Eteokles is "justly famed" (from *eteos*, just, true, and *kleos*, fame), and in the argument with the Chorus about whether or not he will go to the seventh gate, Eteokles dwells on fame and honor as though, in deciding to confront his brother, he hoped to implement this meaning of his name. However, another possible meaning of Eteokles, "truly bewept" or "true cause of weeping" (combining *eteos* with *klaio*, weep), is fearfully suggested in Eteokles' opening speech, and alluded to with increasing dread throughout the play. It suggests to him a fate which he tries with all his powers to evade; hence his prohibition of weeping to the Chorus, and his own refusal to weep when he feels that fate has pointed him toward fratricide at the seventh gate. And just as the measures Oedipus took to avoid the fate spelled out for him at Delphi nevertheless brought about its complete fulfillment, so Eteokles' attempt to avoid the fulfillment of this second, more ominous meaning of his name results in its implementation; as even he himself perhaps begins to recognize when he says,

let the generations of Laios go down to the last man,
blown wind-wracked along the weeping river of Hades.

In the act of killing his brother he finds the answer to the riddle of his own identity and fate, a riddle posed by the double meaning of his name. The second, or buried meaning, "true cause of weeping," "truly bewept," is literally acted out as the Chorus of Theban women, joined by Antigone and Ismene, perform their lament (1044-1280) over the bodies of the brothers who have murdered each other. At this point it is clear that the names and fates of the brothers are interchangeable. Reconciliation and total equality are achieved together. Polyneices is just as "truly bewept" in this scene as Eteokles. In the preceding scene the Chorus warns Eteokles,

do not take on the violence of your brother
of evil name and fame . . .

But by the end of the scene Eteokles has done just that. In deciding to meet his brother at the seventh gate he becomes the counterpart of Ares, the emblem of strife in the house of Laios.

Both in imagery and action the play is an elucidation and dramatic unfolding of these two names. The storm of strife, presided over by Ares and the Fury, is realized in the Argive army outside the walls, and in the Chorus's fearful visualization of the final destruction of Thebes in their second song. The storm of weeping is realized in the Chorus's entrance song as well as in the final lament.

VI

There are many texts, both ancient and modern, that maintain, with elegiac eloquence, that it is the lot of mankind to be born, to suffer, and to die. However sagely we may assent to this universal condition of existence, no particular man likes to think that this is the governing limit of his own life; and when he speaks of his lot, though he may acknowledge it as a limited one, he is inclined at the same time to feel that it entails certain rights and prerogatives, that it is truly and only his, and not to be shared by anyone else. It is therefore associated most easily with what he comes to regard as his just due, his personal fortune, a wealth, either earned or inherited, though that wealth may be expressed in any number of ways, such as strength or courage or a gift for music or telling jokes.

Aeschylus takes the richest possible advantage of these ambiguities in *Seven Against Thebes*; and behind the ambiguities, of course, lie the unresolved problems of free will and justice. That is to say, does a man choose his lot, or is it chosen for him? Does he get what he deserves, and by what or whose standards? While these problems are woven into the background of almost every tragedy, in this drama we are made to take particular notice of them. The first speech of the Scout recounts the drawing of lots. It appears that both Eteokles and Polyneices, while realizing that a part of their inheritance must include their father's Curse, seem also to feel that it includes title to the kingship of Thebes. As for the Curse itself, Eteokles at least seems to feel, when at last he is brought to acknowledge that it cannot be evaded, that it is confined purely to the prophecy that the sons of Oedipus shall divide his wealth with a sword; that is to say, he thinks of the Curse as something laid upon his brother and himself by his father, not as something laid upon his grandfather, his father, and the two brothers in their turn, for the original and continuing violations and crimes of the house. The father's wealth, for which the brothers are prepared to fight to the death, is the city of Thebes, its land, its fecund, life-giving sustenance. What they actually win in their duel is just enough of that land to be buried in. Yet the land is truly a part of their wealth, and indeed of the wealth of all the inhabitants of Thebes; it is life itself. To the Chorus, who are women, this appears to be much clearer than it is to the two ambitious brothers. The Chorus sing movingly about the richness and fertility of the land, and the horror of its despoliation; and their sympathy with the land might perhaps derive from their sharing with it a common gender. At the same time, and perhaps for the same reason, they conceive human life itself as being a form of wealth (372-3):

Our city's wealth of men
climbs to the battlements.

And, again, later (977-9)

The city's wealth,
this heavy freight of men, this swollen horde
must, from the stern, now be cast overboard.

That, as in the Book of Jonah, a forfeit must be paid, some wealth rendered up to protect and preserve the remainder, the mariners on the ship to Tarshish or the inhabitants of Thebes, appears to these women a natural if terrible part of the economy of justice; life must be paid out that life may be sustained. For the two brothers it means, with a disastrous, ultimate irony, that the wealth for which they fight is precisely what they must forfeit: their lives.

Our translation is based on the text of Gilbert Murray, *Septem Quae Supersunt Tragoediae*, Oxford Classical Texts, 2nd ed., 1955. To have acknowledged individually the work of every scholar who has contributed to our understanding of the play would have made the Notes unduly cumbersome. Students of Aeschylus will recognize how great our debt is.

This translation was undertaken in Rome at the American Academy, where we were both the happy beneficiaries of the hospitality of Frank E. Brown, to whom, in gratitude, this work is dedicated.

It was also undertaken at a time when citizens of Aeschylus' native land were suffering (as they continue to, even now) oppression, imprisonment, and torture, for speaking out against the regime that today controls Greece and its culture.

It was undertaken, finally, at a time that can be regarded as possibly the most shameful in our nation's history; in which we have prosecuted a war for which there can be no moral, political, or military justification. A nation can rarely redeem itself from its follies and errors, the cost of which in human misery is incalculable. It is our forlorn but continuing hope that our government may look with some charity upon the young men who thought it from the first a foolish, brutal, and dishonorable undertaking. Our commitment to the work involved in this translation has, in some measure, been colored by these feelings.

Fire Island   HELEN H. BACON
                                                                      ANTHONY HECHT

SEVEN AGAINST THEBES

CHARACTERS

ETEOKLES son of Oedipus, ruler of Thebes
ANTIGONE
ISMENE } sisters of Eteokles
SCOUT a soldier
MESSENGER of magistrates of Thebes, a civilian
KORYPHAIOS Chorus leader
CHORUS of Theban women

Male citizens of Thebes
Magistrates of Thebes
Champions assigned to defend the gates of Thebes:
MELANIPPOS, POLYPHONTES, MEGAREUS, HYPERBIOS, AKTOR, LASTHENES
Theban soldiers
Six slave girls, attendants of Eteokles
Mourning women, attendants of Antigone and Ismene

Line numbers in the right-hand margin of the text refer to the English translation only, and the Notes at p. 72 are keyed to these lines. The bracketed line numbers in the running headlines refer to the Greek text.

An open square on the citadel of Thebes. Three doors with porticos reached by steps—council chamber right, temple center, palace left. In front of the temple a round altar with steps. Grouped around the altar from left to right, statues of Ares in full armor, Athena with aegis, spear, and helmet, Poseidon with trident, Zeus with thunderbolt, Artemis in hunting dress with bow and quiver, Apollo with lyre, Aphrodite with doves.

Enter severally, a crowd of male citizens between the ages of sixteen and sixty—i.e., capable of some kind of military service. Some are armed, some not. Those with weapons stack them, then gather in front of the council chamber.

Enter ETEOKLES *from the council chamber attended by magistrates (men over sixty) of the city of Thebes, in civilian dress. He stands in the portico of the council chamber and addresses the citizens.*

ETEOKLES Citizens, children of Kadmos,
        whoever has charge of affairs in the stern of the ship,
        holding the rudder, sleepless, unblinking,
        must say what has got to be said.
        If things go well for us, it's because of the god.
        If, on the other hand,
        a disaster should strike (which heaven forbid),
        the moiling, the tidal groans, the sea-lamentation
        would sound the name "Eteokles"
        as wail and dirge all through the city.   10
        And I, Eteokles, alone the cause of weeping,
        Eteokles bewept,
        would be multiplied in the surge
        and raving of all your voices,
        and so prove fitly named
        for the city of the Kadmeians.
        May Zeus, Averter, forbid it.

But all of you now must come to assist the city
and the altars of her gods.
The young boy, not yet a man,   20
the one who, past his prime, has already planted
many a sapling child,
and you in the fullness of manhood,
shall each have his function.
So the honor of this mothering land may not be
　　　extinguished,
either for her children whom she brought forth and
　　　cherished,
or for herself, their parent and devoted nurse.
For when you were infants on all fours,
dandled upon her nourishing hills and valleys,
she welcomed the familiar burdens of child-rearing, ·   30
tended you, brought you up, so that
you would be filial keepers of her house,
bearers of shields, and fit
for such need and moment as this is.
Up to this point
the god has inclined the scales in our favor;
so far during this siege the war goes well
in the main, thanks to the gods.
As of this moment our priest, shepherd of birds,
Teiresias, without benefit of light,   40
by ear and by thought alone, sorts out
the omen-giving birds with his trustworthy science;
this lord of divinations keeps saying
that the chiefs of the Achaians, in council all this night,
have planned an attack on our city.
Then, run, all of you,

The citizens rush to pick up their weapons and adjust them.

rush to the battlements and gates of our walls.
Fall out in full armor, crowd to the gunwales,
position yourselves at bow and stern of the towers,

stand firm at the gates, and be of good heart.   50
Do not give in to panic before this mob of outsiders.
It is the god who brings about good conclusions.

A few citizens take command and lead the rest off in
various directions.

SCOUT, *in light armor, runs in from left as the citizens run out.* ETEOKLES
comes down from the steps of the council chamber to meet him.
Magistrates follow at a distance.

But I myself have sent out scouts, sure-footed, clear of eye,
to spy on the camp. Their reports will save me
from all traps and deception.

SCOUT Eteokles, most fittingly king of the Kadmeians,
I come with clear news from beyond the walls,
for I have seen myself all I can tell you.
This night there were seven men, violent, terrible, captains,
they slit the throat of a bull, catching the blood   60
in an inverted shield, bound with black iron.
They splashed their hands in bull blood, they swore
by the trinity of battle, Ares, god of strife,
Enyo, goddess of frenzy, and Phobos, god of fear,
either to sack and gut this city,
or by dying to smear and defile
this life-giving land with their blood.
Tearfully they brought keepsakes to send home to their
        parents
in the event of their deaths
and hung these on the chariot of their general, Adrastos;   70
and though they wept, no one uttered a word of grief,
because courage, an iron passion, gripped them
so that their eyes glared like the eyes of lions,
blazing with Ares.
Scared as I was I kept my head,

watched, made note of these things, and brought you the
    news
as fast as possible. As I was leaving
they were casting lots, each to divine by fortune
against which of our gates he would lead his battalions.
To answer this, therefore, instantly tell off as captains   80
the fittest, the chosen, the most select of the city
for each gate.
Already the Argive hosts in full battle array
are advancing in their own storm of dust.
The mouths of their stallions drip thick foam;
they defile our plowlands.
But like a steady helmsman, you must secure your ship
before Ares strikes in wind and lightning.
The sea-surge of that army shrieks a blood cry.
You must deal with them now and in the readiest way.   90
And I will continue to serve as your distant, enlightening eye
by day, as I have by night,
and informed by the clearness of my reports,
at least when it comes to what is outside our walls,
you will be free from danger and harm.   *Exit left.*

      ETEOKLES *and the magistrates approach the altar and*
      statues of the gods.

ETEOKLES Zeus, Earth, Olympian gods, this city's defenders,
    my father's Curse, and you who will bring it to pass,
    Fury, whose power is great,
    let not this war capsize us
    or overturn our city to ravaged desolation—   100
    our city where the mother tongue of Hellas
    rings in the sanctuary of our homes.
    Do not bind the free city of Kadmos
    in a slave's manacles, but become our defense.
    I should think that I speak in our common cause,
    for only a free and prosperous city
    can make proper gifts to the gods.   *Exeunt into the council*
        chamber.

> *Enter* CHORUS *from left in disorder.*
> *They carry seven garlands and seven robes as offerings*
> *to the gods.*

CHORUS   I shriek fear, a frighted cry of pain.
        The attackers have flooded out of their camp,
        a rushing host, turbulent, thronged with horsemen   110
            foremost.
        A stormcloud of dust in heaven, a voiceless messenger,
        truth-telling but without sound, speaks and convinces.

        Slamming, clashing of steel, hoof-stomp and clubbing
        increase, possess and deafen our land.
        They rumble and thunder
        like a swollen, rock-dashed, hillside torrent.
        Ai, Ai, gods, goddesses,
        avert the swelling storm.

> *They run around wildly, alternately addressing each other*
> *and the statues of the gods.*

        Beyond the walls
        that host with shields like staring eyes   120
        rears, tense and lithe, to spring
        against our city.

        Who will turn them aside? Who will come to our rescue?
        What god? What goddess?
        Shall I fall down before the images of the gods?
        O tranquil, thronèd gods,
        now is the time to clasp your images.
        Why do we stand lamenting when we should be at prayer?

SEMI-CHORUS   Can you hear,
        can you not hear the clanging of shields?   130
        When if not now shall we have recourse to
        supplication with gifts?

SEMI-CHORUS I can see the sound: the hailstone clatter of spears.

> What will you do, Ares?
> Ancestral god of this homeland,
> will you betray it?

> God of the Golden Helmet,
> look, look to the city
> you once chose for your own.

*They form a religious procession, approaching the statue of
each god as he or she is addressed and laying a robe and a
garland at his or her feet.*

CHORUS Now all gods of this land, city's defense,   140
        look down on us, take care
of this pathetic legion of suppliants,
mothers, young brides, virgins who make this prayer,
and stand in danger of slavery, rape, and death.
The helmet crests, blown in the brilliant air,
are foam-froth flung by Ares' lustful breath.
Around this rock, this city, a wind-whipped sea
crashes and roars. O great divinity,
        Zeus, God, Accomplisher, keep out
the enemy, who would bind us with straps and chains.   150
Argives encircle our stronghold. Panic, fear,
terrors of Ares put the soul to rout.
The iron bits, the links of the horses' reins,
ring hard with murder. Seven men, cold breastplates,
        greaves, shields, swords, helmets, and spears,
          each as his lot dictates,
          stand at our seven gates.

        Athena, Zeus' daughter,
lover of battle, become our present balm.
And Lord Poseidon, regent of the water,   160

ruler of sunken hulls and sailors' graves,
tamer of horses, bridler of the waves,
      bring us to harbor's calm.
      And thou, fierce god of strife,
      glad when the battle joins,
Ares, who lives upon the spilling of life,
guard and avow us descendants of your loins
      that fathered Harmonia, Kadmos' wife;
      and Aphrodite, ancestress,
who bore Harmonia in your celestial womb,   170
      give ear to our distress,
hear our petitions, guard us from iron doom.

And thou, Apollo, Lord of Accords, for whom
the wolf in annual sacrifice is slain,
      turn to a wolf against our foes,
with your clear fire drive back the encircling gloom,
      and with your fang disclose
their bitten fear, their boast and purpose vain;
and unwed Artemis, goddess, silver-chaired,
now let your cleansing arrows be prepared.   180

They resume their wild running and exclaiming.

O Artemis, Artemis, the clear heavens are crazed
      with glint and flash of spear.
What will become of the city? Whip and goad
      hasten the clanking chariots.
      They circle us. I hear
shrill scream of ungreased axle under its soldier load.
      Artemis, mistress of untamed beasts,
release us, O relieve us from the cold iron that divides,
      we who observe your feasts.
To what conclusion shall we be   190
      brought by the god that guides?

      Apollo, son of Zeus,
who gives the cleansing ceremony of war,

the pass and purpose of battle, the struggle's use,
I hear at the gates a clanging of brazen shields.
    Huge stones batter our tower-tops,
     a terrible shower falls.
Apollo, foreteller, knower of what awaits,
and blessed Athena, enshrined beyond the walls,
protect, defend this fortress of seven gates.   200

*They return to formal supplication and end up clasping
the images of the gods.*

O governing gods, goddesses who fulfill,
    long honored and adored,
do not betray this city to the will
    of a strangely spoken horde.
Listen, O hear, hear justly these cries, these free
breast-beaten claims upon your sovereignty.

Healers, emancipators, gods who save,
    be partisan, incline
your hearts to remember the offerings we gave,
    harken to this your shrine.   210
Be mindful of future gifts, relieve our groan,
hear our petition, make our cause your own.

Enter ETEOKLES *and magistrates from the council chamber.
He approaches the* CHORUS, *followed by the magistrates,
and addresses the* CHORUS *while they continue to cling to
the images of the gods.*

ETEOKLES You—animals, repulsive beasts—I ask you,
    is this screaming and bawling,
    this hysterical prostration before the shrines
    any way to save our city
    or to encourage defending troops?
    To sane men in command of themselves
    this is an outrage.
    Neither in disaster   220

nor in the careless calm of life
may I ever get cornered and quartered with any female.
When a woman is confident, her insolence can't be endured;
When frightened she's even worse, a danger to house and
     to city.
At this moment, with your storming sea-noise
and your skittering about,
you have drained our souls and paralyzed our citizens,
assisting the tides that threaten our walls:
thus we are being sacked from within.
This is what comes from sharing life with women.   230
And if command is violated by anyone,
man, woman, any who joins with such a one,
the judges shall find against him,
the pebble shall drop its fatal weight on his name,
nor shall he escape his sentence:
to be stoned to death as a traitor at the people's decree.
Outside things are a man's concern.
Let no woman debate them.
You, who belong inside, must stop this havoc and damage.
Can you hear? Can you understand?   240
Or are you beyond comprehension?

CHORUS Beloved son of Oedipus, his dear child,
     I trembled and shook with fear
at the chariots' shaking, the terrible shaking, the wild
     pipe scream, the piercing, clear
panic scream of the axles, and the forged
ringing bits of the horses as they charged.

ETEOKLES Stop. Does the helmsman
who flees to the bow
when the ship is tossed in the swell of the sea   250
find a means of safety
if he lets go of the tiller at the stern?

CHORUS No. But I am a woman, and threw myself
     upon the Blessed Ones,

trusting in them, when a hailstorm seemed to engulf
    the gates with thundering stones.
In terror I cried aloud to them who dwell
above to gird and protect this citadel.

ETEOKLES Then pray that our towers
    stand against the spears of the attack—   260
for this does come from the gods.
There is a saying that
when a city is captured
the gods desert her.

CHORUS O may I die, may I be safely dead
    before the gods remove
from the city, before the sacred gods have fled;
    and may I never live
to see the breaching of walls, the brutal shame
of penetration, the home and shrine aflame.   270

ETEOKLES It is folly to invoke the gods
with such unlucky words.
Submission-to-Proper-Authority
is the Mother-of-Well-Being
and, so men say,
the Wife-of-Him-Who-Saves.

CHORUS True, but the strength of gods is greater than man's,
    and if disaster come
can often lift the weak with invisible hands
    from depths no eye can plumb,   280
from pits of anguish, from the deeps of doubt,
when his own vision is darkened and put out.

ETEOKLES But at the moment of enemy attack
it is for men to slaughter
the sacrificial beast
and to perform divination.

It is for you to remain silent
and to stay indoors.

CHORUS Though the hordes of attacking men be held at bay
                    by strength and the city's towers,   290
            it is the gods alone allot the day;
                    theirs are the holy powers
            to secure our walls, and give us hope to live.
            What cause for anger and hatred could this give?

ETEOKLES I feel no anger
            that you honor the race of gods,
            but you are making our citizens
            faint-hearted with your lamentations.
            Use words of more hopeful omen
            and do not incite to panic.   300

CHORUS Hearing the clashing of armor, the metal ring
                    and cacophony of arms,
            I, a mere woman, came to this place to sing
                    prayers against battle's harms,
            came to the sacred acropolis, in fear
            of strife and bloodshed, came to the citadel here.

ETEOKLES If you hear of men
            dying or wounded,
            do not besiege the city
            with your wailing laments.   310
            For Ares must pasture
            on the murder of mortals.

CHORUS (1st voice) I hear the snorting of horses.

ETEOKLES If you do, act as though you didn't.

CHORUS (2nd voice) The surrounded city groans at its cornerstones.

ETEOKLES This is purely my concern—not yours.

CHORUS (*3rd voice*) I'm frightened: the clangor at the gates swells
and grows louder.

ETEOKLES But you must stop this dangerous noise inside the city.

CHORUS (*4th voice*) O company of gods, do not betray the de-
fenses.

ETEOKLES I don't give a damn what you feel. You must keep quiet 320
and endure.

CHORUS (*5th voice*) Native and citizen gods, don't let me be
taken in slavery.

ETEOKLES But you yourselves are enslaving me and the whole city.

KORYPHAIOS All-powerful Zeus, turn your bolt against the enemy.

ETEOKLES O Zeus, what a race of women you gave us.

KORYPHAIOS Miserable, just as men are, when their city is taken.

ETEOKLES How dare you speak of defeat while touching the images?

KORYPHAIOS Fear has charge of my tongue, and my heart is faint.

ETEOKLES Grant me, I beg, a small favor.

KORYPHAIOS The sooner you speak it, the sooner I can comply.

ETEOKLES Be silent, wretched women; don't panic your friends.   330

KORYPHAIOS I am silent. I will endure with the others what is to come.

ETEOKLES I like these last words better.
Now stand from the images,
and instead of raving,
offer this useful prayer: *The* CHORUS *move away
from the statues.*

"May the gods strengthen our men and direct our spears."
But first, hear my sacred vow;
then raise Apollo's chant, holy, propitious,
a victory cry and halleluiah,
the appropriate ceremonial of Hellas,   340
as at our sacrificial rites,
giving confidence to friends,
letting loose fear to the enemy.   *He approaches the statues*
                                                    of the gods.

I speak to the defending gods of the land
who oversee the plowland and marketplace,
to the springs of Dirke and the waters of Ismenos I speak;
and this I make my vow:
if things turn out well and the city survives,
the sons of Kadmos shall make the altars of the gods
run with blood and slaughter bulls upon them.   350
I will erect trophies, and with enemy spoils, taken by spear,
I will adorn the fronts of the temples, the gods' holy houses.
This is my prayer and vow.
(*To the* CHORUS) Imitate this prayer, without lamentation,
without keening and moaning like beasts.
Whatever is to come will come; your noise can't stop it.
I will go and assign six men, myself the seventh,
all fully armed oarsmen,
against the champions at the seven exit-points of the city
before swift sea-lashing words of a messenger   360
come and ignite new panic.

            Exeunt the magistrates into the council chamber,
        ETEOKLES *right to join the defenders. The* CHORUS *address*
                                                each other.

CHORUS   I will try to do my part,
            to shape my prayer as these formulas require,
            but the pulse of fear will not be lullabyed;

and in the neighboring regions of my heart
anxieties ignite, terrors catch fire,
and agitations, fanned by the blown sound
      of the circling hosts outside,
      smolder and burn. I quake,
like the mild paralyzed dove who, from her perch,   370
huddled with unfledged nestlings all around,
      eyes the thick snake.

      Our city's wealth of men
      climbs to the battlements.
What shall become of us all, our prayers and hopes?
From the enemy skies a hail of jagged stones
whistles and plunges around our defending troops.

They turn and address the gods in a controlled and orderly
                manner.

      O gods from Zeus descended,
may our embattled soldiery and the city
of the descendants of Kadmos enlist your favor   380
and by your invincible powers be defended.

If you abandoned this our deep-soiled ground
      into the enemy hand,
where could you find its equal, where would you go,
      to what dark alien land?

To leave the springs of Dirke, of all sweet waters
      most life-giving and clear
among the gifts of Poseidon and Ocean's daughters!
      O gods, let naked fear,
man-eating cowardice possess our foe   390
      outside the walls. Implant
panic that makes men drop their arms and run;
      and in our voices grant

a glory to yourselves. Hearing these drones
of lamentation and prayer, knowing the outward danger,
become the city's wardens; secure your thrones.

Their gestures became more excited.

Pitiful and terrible it would be
to deliver so august, so famous a city
  to the Dark House of Death;
brought down in flaking ashes, like a felled beast,
   rent without pity   400
  or honor by the enslaving rod,
  the wooden-shafted spear
hurled by a fellow Hellene, backed by a god;
   and terrible, a pity
for all these women assembled here today,
the withered and white-headed, the young and fair,
to be led off, like horses, by the hair,
   their clothing ripped, their breasts
   exposed to the conqueror's view.
Eviscerated, the stunned city screams.   410
   Ulooloo, Ulooloo
The booty hauled away. Shouts. Brutal jokes.
I quake. I dream the most terrible of dreams.

They leave the statues. For the rest of the ode the sack of
the city is mimed.

O terrible, before a woman is ripe,
without accustomed procession, accustomed song,
to go the awful road from her own home
under the sword's compulsion. I say the man
who dies in battle is better off than this.
For when a city is doomed to armored rape,
blades flash in the firelight; murderers throng   420

the streets. Gigantic Ares, in his bliss,
dazed and insane with the towering flame and fume,
befouls the pieties, harvests his dead wealth,
and breathes from our black smoke his terrible health.

The city echoes with loud, bellowing howls;
it is a death-trap, fatally self-ensnared.
A thin blood-cry of infants, a shrill reed
      of nursling terror wails,
and lumbering spearmen pierce each other's bowels.
      Pillagers loot each other   430
in plundering brotherhood; greed joins with greed;
      the empty-handed hails
with rallying cry his empty-handed brother;
no one content with a lesser or equal share.
Who shall account for this portioning, by what law
comes this allotment of pain, grief, and despair?

It is a bitter sight for the housewife
to see, spilled piecemeal from her cherished store,
the foison and wealth of earth, the harvest riches,
grain, oil, and wine, dashed from their polished jars,   440
      sluicing the filthy ditches.
      And by the rule of strife,
the pale, unfamilied girl become the whore
and trophy of her captor, forced to spread
for the sweating soldier, triumphant, hate-inflamed.
Perhaps a dark deliverance may occur
      in that foul bridal, the untamed
violence of that battle-grounded bed.
      And there may come to her
      a species of relief,   450
an end of tidal groans, weeping, and grief.

CHORUS (1st voice) The spy, the army seer, is bringing us news.
    He is coming in haste, quick-footed, and zealous.

                Enter the SCOUT *from left, running.*

CHORUS (*2nd voice*) And here is the lord himself, the child of
            Oedipus,
        at the right moment to hear the messenger,
        equally swift and full of zealous purpose.

> *Enter* ETEOKLES *from right, also in haste, attended by a*
> *group of armed men—six captains, each with a small*
> *company of foot-soldiers.*

SCOUT I speak, with knowledge, of matters outside,
        of what lot and what gate each champion drew.
        Tydeus already thunders near the gate of Proitos,
        but the priest Amphiaraos will not permit the enemy army   460
        to cross the ford of Ismenos
        because the omens are not propitious.
        But Tydeus, raving and gluttonous for battle,
        bellows like a chimera in noonday clangor.
        He abuses and berates Apollo's priest, Amphiaraos,
        alleging that he licks the hand of fate and avoids battle
        out of cowardice. Shouting such things as this,
        he shakes the three crests of his helmet,
        and, behind the rim of his shield,
        brass-forged bells clash fear.   470
        On the shield itself he bears this top-lofty blazon:
        heaven forged with flaming stars, and at the center
        the triple goddess of the three ways,
        a brilliant full moon, the most revered,
        the queen of all the stars, the eye of night,
        stands out, embossed.
        And now, raving and brandishing
        this boastful, haughty-blazoned shield,
        he bellows at the banks of the stream,
        lusting for battle,   480
        like a horse that, hearing the brazen horn-blast,
        snorts in rage at his bridle, rears and stamps.
        Whom will you send against this man?
        When the bars of the gate of Proitos are drawn,
        who will stand firm in that place?

ETEOKLES I am not overcome by the trappings of any man.
Blazons don't wound.
Crests and bells lose their sting, without spears.
And this midnight, shining with heavenly stars
on the shield that you speak of,   490
perhaps this dark folly will be an oracle for someone.
For if it should fall upon his eyes in death,
then the boastful device would be named,
fittingly and with justice,
darkness for him who carries it.
And he himself
against himself
will become his own oracle of impious violence.
But I shall station against Tydeus,
to stand firm at the gate, this man,   500
the worthy son of Astakos,
named "the black horse," Melanippos,

MELANIPPOS *steps forward, followed by his men.*

a noble man who honors the throne of Reverence,
a hater of arrogant words.
He is slow in all shameful practices,
avoiding what is base and cowardly.
He is a thorough son of this land,
a shoot sent up from the seed of the dragon's teeth
sown by Kadmos, and by Ares spared,

MELANIPPOS *holds up his shield with the image of Ares*
on it.

therefore genuinely of our soil.   510
Of course, the chances of battle are as dice in the hands of
        Ares.
But Dike, goddess of all orders, of justice human and divine,
his blood-sister, shall send him forth
to fend off the enemy spear from the mother who bore him.

MELANIPPOS *and his men salute first* ETEOKLES, *their commander, then all the gods together, last of all the statue of
Ares, under whose sign they fight. They then exeunt right.*

CHORUS May the gods grant good fortune to this one
            who rises in the name
of justice at the city's need, a son
            worthy enduring fame.
Yet I tremble lest I look upon the blood
of those who perish for their kindred's good.   520

SCOUT As you say, may the gods give him good fortune.
Kapaneus drew the lot for the gate of Elektra.
A new breed of giant, larger than Tydeus,
he boasts of something beyond the power of man;
he launches terrible threats at the towers;
may fate not fulfill them.
For he says he will sack the city
whether the gods wish it or not.
And not even Zeus,
striking the earth with giant-slaying lightnings,   530
shall get in his way.
He likens those flashings and thunders
to the quiet warmth of noon.
He bears, as his sign, a naked man
armed with a flaming torch
who is crying out in golden letters,
"I shall burn the city."
Against such a man, who will join in battle?
Who will hold his ground without trembling
against this haughty man?   540

ETEOKLES This boast of gain over us will breed our own gains.
The tongues of vain men turn out to be
their clearest accusers.
Kapaneus, fully prepared, threatens to act
in disregard of the gods;
and, running off at the mouth in the joy of vanity,

though a mortal, he directs at heaven
and against Zeus a scathing wave of words.
I firmly believe that the flaming thunder-torch
will come against him in justice—   550
and not as a mere likeness, but the god's torch itself.
Loud-mouthed though he is
a man is chosen to stand against him,
a torch of courage, a mighty man, Polyphontes,

POLYPHONTES *steps forward, followed by his men.*

"killer of many." By the good will of Artemis,
whose shrine stands at that gate,
and of the other gods, he will be a firm defense.

POLYPHONTES *holds up his shield with the image of Athena
with helmet, spear, and aegis on it.*

Therefore, name an enemy at another gate.

POLYPHONTES *and his men repeat the ritual performed by*
MELANIPPOS, *except that their final salute is to the statue of
Athena. They then exeunt right.*

CHORUS May he who vaunts so hugely taste the dust;
                may lightning stop him dead   560
        before he mounts my house in bestial lust
                to soil the marriage bed,
        and with long lance gut and despoil my home,
        my penetralia, my dark and sacred room.

SCOUT I name the man at the next gate.
       The third lot leaped from the upturned
       brazen helmet in favor of Eteoklos,
       who is to hurl his squadron against the gate of Neïs.
       His raging horses wheel, snorting in their armored headgear,
       avid to fall on the gate.   570
       Iron whistles at their nostrils

pipe an inhuman noise, filled with animal breathing.
His shield is arrogantly devised.
A man, fully armed, mounts a ladder against the walls
of an enemy, preparing to sack;
and he bellows in lettered speech
that not even Ares could cast him down from the tower.
Against this man assign a firm defender
to fend off the yoke of slavery from this city.

ETEOKLES Here is the man I would send;   580

> MEGAREUS *steps forward, followed by his men.*

and a certain apt fortune goes with him.
Here he is, assigned; his boast is in the strength of his arm;
Megareus, of the seed of Kreon, of the race of sown men.
Unmoved by the thunder
of the snortings of maddened horses,
he will not budge from the gate;

> MEGAREUS *holds up his shield with the image of Poseidon*
> *wielding his trident on it.*

but either by dying will repay his nurture to mother Earth,
or by capturing both a man
and a man and city upon a shield,
he will adorn the home of his father with spoils.   590
Tell me the boast of another—the full, clear facts.

> MEGAREUS *and his men perform the ritual of salutation, end-*
> *ing with the statue of Poseidon, and exeunt right.*

CHORUS O champion of my house, may you fare well,
              and so, for them, fare ill;
        just as they roar against us, rail and yell,
              vaunting their ravening will,
        shouting the blood-theme of their brazen boasts,
        May Zeus Avenger's wrath behold their hosts.

SCOUT Another, the fourth, stationed at the gate of Athena,
comes forward with a shout, the huge
aspect and frame of Hippomedon.   600
The enormous threshing-floor,
that is, the circle of his shield—
I shuddered when he twirled it, I must confess.
The maker of the blazon, whoever it was
embossed that work on his shield,
was no common artisan:
Typhon, breathing fire, black smoke,
sister of glittering fire, pouring from his mouth;
and the border of the hollowed shield
is encoiled with his tail.   610
The man himself yells out his war cry,
and filled with the god Ares, like a very Maenad,
revels in blood-glee, glaring forth fear.
Take thought of the test in meeting such a man,
for Panic is already boasting at that gate.

ETEOKLES First of all, Athena, close neighbor of the city gate,
hating irreverent violence,
will ward off the wintry snake from the nestlings.
Hyperbios, "queller of violence," noble son of Oinops,

HYPERBIOS *steps forward, followed by his men.*

is chosen champion against this contender,   620
a man who wishes to search out his fate
in the extremity of the occasion.
Neither in form, in spirit, nor in the bearing of arms
can he be faulted.
Hermes, by divine reason, has matched this pair;
for this man is the other's natural enemy,
and the gods on their shields are at enmity.
One has fire-breathing Typhon,
but Hyperbios has immovable Zeus, the father,

HYPERBIOS *holds up his shield with the image of Zeus
wielding his thunderbolt on it.*

and vanquisher of Typhon, planted on his shield,   630
and the god bears aloft his flaming lightning dart.
Such are the portents the gods have given each side.
We are clearly on the winning side,
they on the losing,
if Zeus is mightier than Typhon in battle.
Perhaps the two champions will fare accordingly.
To Hyperbios, by his own blazon,
Zeus would become a savior,
being, by good fortune, upon his shield.

       HYPERBIOS *and his men perform the ritual of salutation,*
          ending with the statue of Zeus, and exeunt right.

CHORUS Certain I am that he who bears as crest   640
        the anti-type of Zeus,
  the hideous earth god, serpentine, unblessed,
        with whom there is no truce
in lasting enmity of gods or men,
shall fall before our gates, nor rise again.

SCOUT May it be so. And now I name the fifth,
    stationed at the fifth, the Northern gate,
    beside the tomb of Amphion, of the race of Zeus.
    He swears by the blade he carries—
    revering it above god and his own eyes—   650
    that he will gut the citadel of the Kadmeians
    in spite of Zeus.
    Thus speaks the fair-faced whelp of Atalanta,
    his mother, huntress in the wilderness;
    he is a man with the beauty of a boy,
    the down just visible on his cheeks, the soft beginnings
    of what will be a shaggy mane as his youth flourishes.
    He does not stand before the gates without a boast,
    for on his bronze-bound shield,
    his masking metal riddle and device,   660
    he wields the shame of this city, the Sphinx,

eater of raw flesh, clamped to the shield with bosses,
a shining, hammered body,
pinning down a Kadmeian in her claws.
He means to make a target of himself,
attracting most of our weapons
to himself and the vanquished man upon his shield.
There he stands, with brilliant eye but savage mind
unsuited to his name, Parthenopaios,
"maiden-faced," the Arcadian, not Argive-born,   670
yet repaying his fair and recent nurture
to Argos as if she were his mother.
Having come this far, such a man is not likely to stint
in his carnage, nor let so long a journey
repay him less than it's worth.
May Zeus avert the horrors with which he threatens our
    walls.

ETEOKLES If only they could feel at the hands of the gods
the things that they dream against us
in their unholy boasts,
they would be flatly and totally destroyed.   680
Against this one also, the one you call the Arcadian,
a man is set who does not boast
but his hand sees what must be done,
Aktor, "the doer," brother of him who was named before.

           AKTOR *steps forward, followed by his men.*

He will not permit an unbridled tongue,
flowing within the gates, to breed evils,
nor will he permit
the bite of that most hateful beast
to get from outside in.
That beast will blame the man who carries her   690
when she feels the thick shower of weapons

        AKTOR *holds up his shield with the image of Artemis,*
               huntress, drawing her bow on it.

under the city walls.
With the help of the gods,
I, too, may rightly answer her riddle.

AKTOR *and his men perform the ritual of salutation, ending
with the statue of Artemis, and exeunt left.*

CHORUS My hair rises. The impious message daunts
　　　　　my heart and mind again.
May the undoubted gods, hearing these vaunts
　　　　　of loud, unholy men,
wipe them from earth forever, stop the breath
of blasphemous mouths in slack and silent death.   700

SCOUT I name the sixth.
The most restrained in spirit and the best,
the priest, strong Amphiaraos,
stationed at the Homoloian gate.
He rebukes Tydeus,
who drew the first of the lots,
calls him, "man-slayer, city's bane,
a disastrous counselor to Adrastos
king of the Argives,
a mighty teacher of evil to Argos,   710
conjuror of the Fury, a servant of murder."
And then he calls on your brother,
whose heritage and fate you share,
strong Polyneices,
and repeatedly sounds the ending of his name,
which means "strife."
And this is his pronouncement:
"How can the gods delight in such a deed?
How can posterity admire it,
to sack your father's city and your native gods,   720
launching a foreign force against them?
What natural or divine law, what Dike,
could sanction the quenching of the maternal spring
and source of your life?

How can your mother land, wife to your father,
ravaged by your lust and looming spear,
accept and espouse you?
But this land that you would make your enemy
shall open and take me into her bosom,
take me, Apollo's priest—so I foresee 730
and hide me from this violence and desecration;
and I shall make her fertile.
Let the battle begin.
The fate I expect is not without honor."
So speaks the priest
as he deftly wields his shield of solid bronze;
its circle carries no device,
because he does not wish to seem best
but in fact to be the best,
harvesting the fruit of his great mind and heart 740
where good counsels take root and flourish.
Against this man I recommend you send
a wise and good oarsman.
The man who honors the gods is a dangerous adversary.

ETEOKLES Alas for the mortal fortune that links
one just man with an impious mob.
There is nothing worse
than wicked companions; no fruit is reaped therefrom.
The field of Ate, of self-will,
yields a harvest only of death. 750
A reverent man aboard a ship
of hot-headed sailors or pirates
perishes with that god-rejected race of men.
When men lose their humanity and forget the gods
they are obliged to suffer the Fury's lash.
A just man in their company
is caught in the same trap, though without deserving.
He is marked and damned.
So the priest Amphiaraos, a man
of self-control, a just man, good and reverent, 760
and a great prophet, is joined with unholy

bold-mouthed men against his better judgment,
men who have come too far to turn back now.
If the god so decrees, he shall be dragged down with them.
Perhaps he will not even attack the gates—
not because he lacks courage, or is base in spirit,
but he knows how he must end in battle,
if the prophetic saying of Apollo bear fruit.
Still, I shall station a man against him,
mighty Lasthenes, a gate-keeper who hates outsiders.   770

> LASTHENES steps forward, followed by his men.

In mind a man of many years, youthful in flesh and bodily
    form,
with a swift-footed eye, a quick-witted hand
to divine with keen spear-point

> LASTHENES holds up his shield with the image of Apollo
> on it.

the unarmored, naked patch of flesh
under the masking shield.
But good fortune for mortals
is a gift of the god alone.

> LASTHENES and his men perform the ritual of salutation,
> ending with the statue of Apollo, and exeunt left.

CHORUS O gods, hear our just entreaties, stem the attack,
     take part in this our strife.
Turn the invader's spear-point evils back   780
     even against his life.
May Zeus thunder against him, may he fall
under the god's fierce bolts outside the wall.

SCOUT The seventh man at the seventh gate—I name him now:
your own brother. And you shall know what Curses
he calls down upon the city

and what fate he vows for it.
He declares he will scale and bestride the walls,
proclaimed lord and subjugator of the land.
Yelling his full-lunged victory song   790
over the trapped and the beaten,
he will fight you hand to hand;
and either, in killing you, lie dead beside you,
or else drive you into dishonored exile
just as you forced such banishment on him.
This is what he bellows,
and calls on the gods of our mother land,
wife to his father, begging them to
be wardens of his fortunes—
this mighty Polyneices.   800
He has a newly forged, perfect-circled shield,
and clamped on it a twofold device.
A stately woman guides forward a warrior
in full armor who is hammered out in gold.
She says she is Dike—goddess of all orders,
human and divine—
and inscribed there are these words:
"I shall bring this man to his harbor
and he shall enjoy his father's city,
shall tumble and make free with his house."   810
Such are the engines of the enemy.
Now you alone can decide whom it is best to send.
If there's a fault to be found
in the situation, it is not with my report.
Now you alone can decide how best to pilot this vessel.

                                                    Exit left.

ETEOKLES God-hated, hateful, beaten and trapped,
          O god-maddened, O race of Oedipus,
          ringed round with hate my patrimony, full of tears;
          the Curses of my father once again
          bring forth a sickening fruit.   820
          But no weeping now; no lamentation.
          They could engender a greater and wider grief.

Polyneices, full of strife, much striven over,
you are well named. Soon we will know
how his blazon and device will do its work—
whether in fact the gold-incised letters on the shield
will bring the babbling, aberrated brother to his harbor.
If Dike, maiden daughter of Zeus,
had been present in the deeds and heart of this man,
perhaps it might come about.   830
But neither when he fled from the darkness of his mother,
nor at the breast, not as a boy,
nor when his first beard began
did Dike ever look upon him, or find him
worthy of her company.
Then she is not likely to be at his side
or help him in this violence,
this crime against the parent land.
If she did she would be, quite justly,
falsely named Justice; linked with a man   840
who would dare anything.
Trusting in this, I shall go;

*He steps forward alone into the place where the other
champions stood.*

I shall stand against him myself.
Who has a juster claim than I?
Ruler against ruler, brother against brother,
hater against hater, I must take my rightful place.
Quickly, bring my armor,

*One of the remaining soldiers steps up to the door of the
palace, opens it, and makes a summoning gesture to those
within.*

the masking metal riddle to ward off stones and spears.

CHORUS Son of Oedipus, dear to this land,
         do not take on the violence of your brother   850

of evil name and fame. Surely it is enough that the
    Kadmeians
fight at close quarters with the Argives;
there is a ritual of purification
for the spilling of such blood.
O but of this consanguinity,
of two men who share the same blood,

*Enter from the palace six slave girls, each carrying a piece
of armor—greaves, breastplate, sword and sword belt, helmet, shield (held so that the inner side faces the audience),
spear. They stand in the portico of the palace holding the
arms in front of them.*

the death of one by the hand of the other
who is the image of himself—
such blood spills pollution which endures
and fouls beyond cleansing.   860

ETEOKLES If a man's lot be to suffer evil, let it be without shame.
    That is our only gain when we are dead.
    But take note that there is neither glory
    nor gain when shame and misfortune go together.

Slave girl helps him buckle on greaves.

CHORUS Why this mad eagerness in you, my child?
    Do not be borne away now by the flood
    of blind, spear-maddened rage, heart-swollen and wild.
    Cast out this corrupting lust now and for good.

ETEOKLES Since the Fury brutally forces on the event,
    let the generations of Laios go down to the last man,   870
    blown wind-wracked along the weeping river of Hades,
    even as is their lot, right from the first,
    being hated of Phoibos, branded and unclean.

Slave girl helps him buckle on breastplate.

CHORUS A stinging desire, like a poisoned fly,
 bites at you even to the mind's dark root,
 goads to a man-lopping harvest, a crimson dye
 of unlawful blood, a vile and bitter fruit.

ETEOKLES It is true. The hateful Fury, the black Curse
 of my beloved father has picked out its meat.
 It settles down with dry and tearless eyes.   880
 It speaks of a gain to be had from a doom that will follow.

Slave girl helps him buckle on sword.

CHORUS Resist this voice. A prosperous career
 and prudent is thought cowardly by no man.
 No black cyclonic Fury will appear
 when the gods accept a sacrifice at your hands.

ETEOKLES Somehow, for a long time,
 We have ceased to be a concern of the gods.
 Our death is the only sacrifice they would value.
 Why any longer lick
 at the bone hand of man-harvesting Fate?   890

Slave girl helps him buckle on helmet.

CHORUS Now, while the storm towers about you, wait;
 hold back, consider, before the day is lost.
 In time the wind-swept goddess, the cold Fate,
 might veer more gently. Now she is tempest-tossed.

Slave girl offers the shield to ETEOKLES, *still with inner side
facing the audience.* ETEOKLES *fits his arm through the grips
of the shield, then turns and holds it up so that the audience can see the device—the Fury.*

ETEOKLES She is tempestuous because my father's Curse
 opened again like a pustule. They were all too true,

51

those omens that came in dreams, those whisperings
of the wealth of Oedipus, split by an iron sword.

KORYPHAIOS Though it is hard for you, be persuaded by women.

ETEOKLES Then speak only of what can be done, and to the point.   900

KORYPHAIOS Do not go that road to the seventh gate.

> *Slave girl hands* ETEOKLES *the spear. Exeunt slave girls into
> palace.* ETEOKLES *holds up the spear.*

ETEOKLES Your words cannot blunt me, whetted as I am.

KORYPHAIOS And yet there are victories without glory,
and the gods have honored them.

ETEOKLES These are no words for a man in full armor.

> *Takes the same attitude as the statue of the god, Ares,
> behind him.*

KORYPHAIOS Can you wish to harvest your very brother's blood?

ETEOKLES If the gods dispose evil, no man can evade it.

> ETEOKLES *salutes all the statues of the gods as a group and
> exits left, running. The remaining soldiers stand in con-
> fusion for a moment, then exeunt left more slowly.*

> *The* CHORUS *group themselves around the altar and deliver
> the following ode with relatively little movement.*

CHORUS I shudder at this goddess, home-wrecker,
true oracle of evils and of doom,
foreteller of the worse,   910
the ordained aftermath;
so unlike all the gods, this mighty Fury

      the father called upon.
I fear that she is working out the wrath
of unhinged Oedipus in his dark frenzy
      who spoke the awful Curse.
An ancient blood-strife, a child-murdering
inheritance, and terrible heirloom
of folly and disobedience drives these brothers on.

It is savage-minded iron, the Chalybian stranger,   920
Scythian immigrant Ares doles out their lot,
a bitter executor of the family wealth.
From his great shaken helmet he plucks out
the scrap that says they shall dwell in as much land
as the dead may need, and have no part or share
in the wide fields, sweet waters, the living air.

When these self-slaughterers lie
in mutual murder pierced,
and the dry dust of earth
with parched, inhuman thirst   930
drinks up the criminal blood
where it leaks, black and clotted,
who would perform the rites
that purify, would wash
the hacked and ruined limbs?
New miseries for this house
mixed now with furious evils
anciently allotted.

I speak of an old breach
of law, long since begotten,   940
but bitterly swift to bring
retributive disaster;
and yet it lingered on
to the third generation.
Three times the Lord Apollo
in the midmost Pythian navel,
the prophetic center, spoke:

if Laios were to live
childless, without issue,
then the city would be safe. 950
But madly overcome
by lust, the body's folly,
despite the speaking god
Laios begot his doom,
the father-slaying son,
King Oedipus, who sowed
his outrageous agony
in the inviolate field
of his mother, the same womb
that bore and cherished him; 960
and planted there in blood
the wrath-bearing root.
Madness, mind-shattering,
brought bride and groom to bed.

Like a plunging and storm-agitated sea,
        disaster drives the wave;
first one wave falls, a second rises up,
a third, three-crested, crashes at the stern
        of the city in angry foam.
        Between our perilous home 970
        and total jeopardy,
our hull is the mere width of the city walls.
I fear shipwreck, I fear unspeakable things,
the city's destruction, the foul death of two kings.

Busy destruction will not spare these two.
A heavy settlement of ancient curses comes
inexorably home. The city's wealth,
this heavy freight of men, this swollen horde
must, from the stern, now be cast overboard.

For who was so marveled at 980
by the very gods themselves,
by those who shared with him

the self-same city hearths,
by the generations of men
that populate the earth,
or by them so much honored
as Oedipus, the king,
destroyer of the Sphinx,
that man-destroying fate
crouching upon our land?   990
But when he realized,
poor man, the nature and truth
of his impossible marriage,
then, raving in agony,
he brought two crimes to pass.
With father-slaying hand
he tore out his own eyes,
more valuable to him
than the sight of his two sons,
who were hateful to his eyes.   1000
And then, against these sons,
in wrath at twisted lineage,
he launched these bitter-tongued
Curses: that in due time
they should be dealt their wealth
with a hand that wields cold iron.
I tremble, I fear, lest this
should now be brought to pass
by the fleet-footed Fury.

> *Enter* SCOUT, *running, from left.*
> CHORUS *cluster around him.*

SCOUT Take heart, you need not fear   1010
  the horrors reserved for women in war.
  The city has been delivered from the yoke of slavery.
  The boastings of storming men have fallen to the ground.
  The city rides at calm; we have shipped no water.
  The walls were sea-worthy, and we shored up our gates
  with firm combatants and defenders.

In the main, things go well at six of the gates.
But Apollo, the holy Lord of Sevens, Lord of Accords,
took as his own the seventh gate,
bringing to completion for the race of Oedipus   1020
the ancient follies of Laios.

KORYPHAIOS What further awful news have you got to tell us?

SCOUT The men are dead, slain by each other's hands.

KORYPHAIOS What men? What did you say?
            You're driving me mad with fear.

SCOUT Take hold of yourself and listen. The race of Oedipus . . .

KORYPHAIOS Woe unto me, I foresaw this evil.

SCOUT Incontestably brought low . . .

KORYPHAIOS Did they come to that? Go on; speak your heavy things.

SCOUT The city is safe, but the two kings of one blood   1030
       have spilled their shared stream out. Earth has drunk up
       the blood of their mutual slaughter. So they were hewn,
       felled at the same moment by brother-hands.

KORYPHAIOS So fatally equal was the spirit they shared.
            So utterly has it consumed the ill-fated race.

SCOUT This is occasion both for rejoicing and weeping—
       that the city fares well, but that those who stand
       over the city, the two generals,
       shared out by lot their full inheritance
       with hammered Scythian iron. So they shall have   1040
       what they won: to be buried in earth,
       who were so ill-fatedly carried away
       on the wind of their father's prayer.   *Exit right.*

The CHORUS *turn to the statues of the gods.*

CHORUS O city-defending gods who oversee
these towers of Kadmos,
shall I rejoice and raise a victory cry
to Zeus, the city's savior,

Enter from left a cortège of soldiers carrying the bodies of
ETEOKLES *and* POLYNEICES *on litters. The* CHORUS *face*
them as they advance.

or shall I instead bewail
the pitiful, unkindly-godded,
and hatefully misbegotten warriors; 1050
who, out of grave, unholy motives,
perished in clear accordance with their names:
Eteokles, true cause of weeping,

Soldiers set down body of ETEOKLES *on right of altar.*

and Polyneices, full of strife?

Soldiers set down body of POLYNEICES *on left of altar.*
The CHORUS *stand over the bodies, making ritual gestures*
of mourning.

O black, conclusive prayer of Laios' race,
Oedipal Curse, O dark.
An evil coldness whelms round, laps at my heart.
When I heard of the leaking corpses, terribly fated
to this polluted death,
like a Maenad, I contrived a melody 1060
and chant of burial.
But what grim, ominous harmony was made
by these brothers in their concert of the spear!

The word invoked by the father, the potent word
went its unwearied way

and was acted out, bloodily, to the last.
The defiant act conceived in Laios' day
           has pierced from the buried past
into their midst and bodies, has pierced through.
           Ulooloo, ulooloo.   1070
Therefore I fear for the city, soiled with this blood.
Nothing can blunt the prophecies of the god.

You two who now lie dumb and strengthless here
defied the pieties, and like bad seed begot
only this barren groan, this sterile tear,
and these distracted words to mourn your lot.
You were yourselves misfortune's instruments,
the silenced theme infecting these laments.

SEMI-CHORUS Articulate these slack and wordless mouths;
           to the eye they are the speech of a messenger;   1080
           here lie our double griefs, a deathly couple,
           twin-fated ancient sorrows, ancestral errors
           mutually murdering, brought to this dark conclusion.

           What shall I say? What is there to be said
           but that these are woes come home, to dwell at the hearth
           and share a bed with the ancient woes of this house.

SEMI-CHORUS But, dear ones, sisters, row
           an escorting funeral oarbeat
           with our head-smiting hands
           down the cold winds of wailing   1090
           to bear away the dead
           across dark Acheron
           like a sacred, black-sailed ship
           of grief, on expedition,
           sailing the sunless way
           untrodden by Apollo
           to the all-welcoming,
           the unseen, bitter shore.

Enter from the palace ANTIGONE *and* ISMENE *followed by a
group of women making gestures of mourning. The* CHORUS
*make room for the procession to take a stand about halfway
between the palace door and the biers.*

CHORUS   For that ungrateful task,
          the lament of these two brothers,   1100
          here now come these two,
          Antigone and Ismene.
          They will surely utter
          loud, unstinted grief
          from lovely breast and throat.
          But it is right for us
          before we hear their voices
          to chant the grating hymn,
          the harsh hymn of the Fury,
          and over the dead to sing   1110
          the hate-filled paean of Hades.

          O in your brothers most unfortunate,
          of all women swayed to the menstrual pulse
                  most luckless and set apart,
                  I groan and weep for you;
          without riddle or mask, but openly
          I make these shrill sounds in the blood of my heart.

The CHORUS *stand near the biers, alternately addressing*
ETEOKLES *and* POLYNEICES, ANTIGONE *and* ISMENE, *and each
                                                    other.*

SEMI-CHORUS   And you, defiant ones, foes to your kindred,
               enemies to yourselves, your family's blood,
               perverse and obstinate in evil paths   1120
               who seized at spear-point what had been your father's,
               O full of grief, unfortunates, who found
               in the deep violation of your home
               misfortune, and the angry, fatal wound;

who pierced the very walls of your own house,
      breached, hacked and defiled,
to taste the sweet prerogative of rule
      and solitary might,
at last, by iron, you are reconciled.

The words of your father, of King Oedipus,   1130
were made true sayings by the listening Fury
who brought these things to pass.
Here two young men lie, pierced through the left side;
the lungs are pierced that once in darkened waters,
unbreathing, floated calm in the same womb.

SEMI-CHORUS Ai, Ai, alas for those Curses brought about
by divine intervention of the gods.
Yet you speak only of these two thrust down,
invaded, pierced in their bodies and their homes
because of an unholy, kindling wrath   1140
and even-handed fate, a father's gift.
But O our city also has been cleft,
cut through with groans. The very towers groan.
Earth groans, the mothering earth that fosters men.
To others there still remain holdings of land,
pasture and fold for those who are still to come,
their possession, the sweet earth. It was for this,
for this that there came to these ill-fated ones
the strife that linked them, the consummation of death.
With hearts like blades, these two young men shared out   1150
this inheritance in just and equal lots.

CHORUS To kindred, bonded in blood to these two men,
the justice of their reconciler, Ares,
is stern, forbidding, costly, without beauty.
Struck down by the god's iron and their own hands,
it is likely that in time someone will ask
what portion of a father's tomb they share
who spilled each other's blood, his blood, with iron.

A chill, echoing wail, "Eteokles,
Heart-Cleaver, Sea of Tears, Eteokles!" 1160
      A very groan of woe,
joyless and savage-minded, weeping salt
from the sickened spirit, rises from their house,
and makes me, in my wailing, waste away
      for the sake of these two lords.

SEMI-CHORUS Of these contentious young it can be said
they altered the fortunes of many in their city
and marshaled into the bloody ranks of death
many who lie full-length in the fields outside.

SEMI-CHORUS O most unfortunate in her hovering god 1170
was she who gave them birth; unfortunate
above all women brought to bed of a child.
Making a husband of her own first-born,
she brought forth these, his brothers, whose brothering
    hands,
warmed in the same recess, dark womb and blood,
came to their limit and last in mutual slaughter.

SEMI-CHORUS Sperm-linked, twinned in the seed, united
      in wrath and loveless strife,
these rivals went to school their killing hatred
      in the first waters of life; 1180
in bowels and belly, in the narrow tubes
      of birth they nursed their wrath,
madness of blade-wounds, hidden ravagement
      brought to this aftermath;
unstrung their limbs in which all strife is spent.

CHORUS Their hatred now is ended, and their lives
      spilled on their mother earth,
where pitifully their only blood lies pooled,
      calm, and of nothing worth.
Truly, at last, they share one common blood. 1190

Ares, that bitter settler of strife,
is the guest foretold from across the hostile sea,
the fire-born, whetted iron of prophecy.
Bitter is Ares, Lord Apportioner,
who dealt such balanced bounty, equal lots,
making the father's furious wish come true.

SEMI-CHORUS They have won the lot they drew
                    at the hands of fate,
God-given lot of sorrow,
                    gift of hate.   1200
Under the body lies
                    the wealth it seized:
the plumbless deeps of earth,
                    silent, appeased.

CHORUS O they have burst into bloom,
they blossom, unfold like petals,
these twin red flowers of a family grief!
Now that the seed of this line, the race of Laios,
                    has turned on itself, and turned
everything into overturning flight,   1210
the sharp-tuned cry of triumph, the victory earned,
                    belongs by evident right
                    but to the Curses.

Only the trophy of Ate, of blindness, stands
                    firm at the fatal gate
where these two perished at each other's hands.
                    The Fury's strength and hate,
having wrought the wills of men, the god's commands,
                    begins now to abate.

The CHORUS *draw back as* ANTIGONE *and* ISMENE *and their
                    attendants come and stand over the bodies.*

ANTIGONE Stricken, you struck back . . .   1220
    ISMENE But died as you cut him down.

ANTIGONE With a spear you slew . . .
ISMENE But by a spear you died.
ANTIGONE Pitiful in your struggle.
ISMENE Pitiful in your suffering.
ANTIGONE Give vent to the wail.
ISMENE Open the sluice of the tear.
ANTIGONE You are stretched out for good . . .
ISMENE Having done murder.

ANTIGONE E, e, 1230
ISMENE E, e,
ANTIGONE My mind is unhinged with wailing.
ISMENE My heart groans in my body.
ANTIGONE Io, Io, thou all-wept for.
ISMENE Thou, also, all-striving.
ANTIGONE You perished by the hand of one who is dear . . .
ISMENE And slew one who is kin.
ANTIGONE A double grief to croon.
ISMENE A double grief to see.
ANTIGONE Here lies sorrow beside brother sorrow. 1240
ISMENE Here stand sisters of those sorrows.

CHORUS Terrible, ungenerous is Fate,
and so are you, dark shade of Oedipus,
lady, whose gifts are cruel pain and weight,
black and abiding Fury, whose power is great.

ANTIGONE E, e,
ISMENE E, e,
ANTIGONE (to POLYNEICES) Sorrows unbearable to the eye . . .
ISMENE Were revealed to me in his return from exile.
ANTIGONE And though he killed, he didn't even get home . . . 1250
ISMENE But as he got within reach of his goal, he perished.
ANTIGONE (to ETEOKLES) And this one also breathed his last . . .
ISMENE And killed this one.
ANTIGONE Pitiful race . . .
ISMENE Which pitifully suffered . . .
ANTIGONE Hard-groaning cares, mourners of like name . . .

ISMENE   Which drowned three generations in a flood of grief.

CHORUS   Terrible, ungenerous is Fate,
and so are you, dark shade of Oedipus,
lady, whose gifts are cruel pain and weight,   1260
black and abiding Fury, whose power is great.

ANTIGONE   You know her, having passed through her terrors.
ISMENE   You, also, learned her ways, no later than he . . .
ANTIGONE   When you came home to the city . . .
ISMENE   As a rival oarsman to his spear.
ANTIGONE   Hopeless to speak.
ISMENE   Helpless to see.
ANTIGONE   Alas for suffering.
ISMENE   Alas for evil.
ANTIGONE   For the house . . .   1270
ISMENE   For the land . . .
ANTIGONE   Above all, for me . . .
ISMENE   And no less for me.
ANTIGONE   Io, Io, of all men, most full of struggle, Polyneices, my
lord . . .
ISMENE   Io. Io, lord of harsh, groaning evils, Eteokles, my ruler . . .
ANTIGONE   Io, Io, possessed by spirits of blindness . . .
ISMENE   Io, Io, where shall we lay them in earth?
ANTIGONE   Io, Io, where they have most right to be . . .
ISMENE   Io, Io, two griefs to sleep beside the father,
and share the father's bed.   1280

Enter MESSENGER *of the magistrates of Thebes, in civilian
dress, from council chamber.*

MESSENGER   I am commanded to announce
the decreed resolution voted
by the magistrates of this City of Kadmos,
and their present pleasure, as well.
They determined to bury this man, Eteokles,
with honor and pomp, in recognition
of his good will toward the land;

for he contained the enemy,
and, in choosing death at the gates of the city
to protect the sanctities of his father,   1290
he was brought to a blameless death.
To die for such things is noble in the young.
I have been told to speak accordingly of this man.
His brother here, the corpse of Polyneices,
I am commanded to say, is to be cast out,
unburied, a thing for dogs to tear at,
because, as they choose to put it, he would
have driven from their lawful homes
the people of Kadmos, if one of the gods
had not thwarted his spear.   1300
Even in death he shall suffer contamination
from the gods of his father, which he dishonored
in trying to bring an outside force within,
and to sack the city. It therefore seems to them right
that this man receive what he deserves:
to be buried only by the winged birds,
without honor.
And there shall not follow him any hands
pouring earth to make a tomb, nor shall he be
honored with shrill songs of mourning,   1310
or borne away by any cherishing kindred.
Such were the things decreed by those
in authority over the Kadmeians.

ANTIGONE I tell those who stand in authority
over the Kadmeians:
if no one else is willing to bury this man,
I shall bury him;
and shall take upon myself any danger
that may be incurred.
Nor am I ashamed to show this defiance   1320
against the city.
Dreadful and terrible, the common entrails
from which we both have come:
from an unfortunate mother and miserable father.

And so my willing soul
shares in my brother's unwilling evil,
and living,
shares his dead misery,
being like-hearted, born of the same bowels.
On this man's flesh no famished wolf shall feast;   1330
let no one decree it.
For I myself, though only a woman,
shall contrive the digging and the funeral rites,
drag him, if need be,
in the folds of my cloak, to the grave of his father and
       brother.
But I shall cover him. Let no man command otherwise.
This shall be done; a way shall be found to do it.

MESSENGER I enjoin you, do not show this defiance to the city.

ANTIGONE I enjoin you, do not come to me with extravagant
proclamations.

MESSENGER A people is harsh toward the contriver of misfortunes   1340
from which they have just escaped.

ANTIGONE Let them be harsh, but this man will not go unburied.

MESSENGER Will you honor in funeral one whom the city hates?

ANTIGONE Have not the gods already determined
that he should inherit his native earth?

MESSENGER So to decide before he cast this land in peril
could not have been just.

ANTIGONE Suffering, he answered with evil.

MESSENGER But he did this deed against all, instead of one.

ANTIGONE I shall bury this man. Don't lengthen the argument.   1350

MESSENGER Be self-willed, but I forbid the act.

Exit into council chamber.

ANTIGONE Last of the gods, the Fury, sower of discord,
has still the last word.

CHORUS O vaunting, blood-corrupting spirits of doom,

*The soldiers form two groups, one with ISMENE around the
bier of ETEOKLES, the other with ANTIGONE around the bier
of POLYNEICES.*

Furies, who shattered the line of Oedipus,
              once proud in the guiding stern,
what will become of me? Where now will I turn?
How could I summon the hardness, the brutal hate
not to lament you and bear you to the tomb?
              And yet I hesitate   1360
in fear and awe of the magistrates' command.
              It is the lot and right
of one of you to have many a mourning voice
              to sing you to your grave,
but the other is denied song, tomb and all
but one sole mourner to lament his fall.
O who would dare follow her path and choice?

Half the CHORUS join ANTIGONE. The other half join ISMENE.

SEMI-CHORUS Whether or not the city rage and cry
              against the pitiful mourners of this man,
              we will bring Polyneices to his grave   1370
              and help you bury him. The grief for kindred
              is the bond and link of mankind, common to all,
              unchanging. Whereas the city declares
              now one thing, now another, to be just.

SEMI-CHORUS But we will go with this one, whom the city
             and Justice both join and delight in praising.
             For second only to the blessed gods,
             to mighty Zeus, this one man most of all
             defended the city of Kadmos, kept the ship
             steady against capsize, guiding it through   1380
             the breakers, the swamping waves of men from without.

             Soldiers pick up biers. POLYNEICES *is carried out left, fol-*
             lowed by ANTIGONE *and* SEMI-CHORUS. ETEOKLES *is carried*
                 out right, followed by ISMENE *and* SEMI-CHORUS.

NOTES AND GLOSSARY

NOTES

A NOTE ON PRODUCTION

The play was produced at the festival of the Greater Dionysia (the principal occasion for the performance of tragedies in Athens) in 467 B.C. As was the custom, it was joined with two other tragedies to form a trilogy—*Laios, Oedipus, Seven Against Thebes*—and followed by a satyr play—a burlesque of a tragedy with a chorus of satyrs—the *Sphinx*. As was also the custom, the author wrote the music to which the lyrics were sung, trained the chorus, directed the actors, and played one of the speaking parts. Under such conditions of production, stage directions and indications about properties and non-speaking parts (what Aristotle in the *Poetics* called spectacle, *opsis*) were superfluous, and none have come down to us. Those supplied in this version represent what we consider the minimum of visual effects necessary to make the play intelligible in production. Some of these, such as the statues of the gods which Eteokles rebukes the Chorus for touching, are explicitly demanded by the text. Others, such as the shield devices of the defenders, are more controversial, but seem to us justified as a means of showing in action how the emblems of attackers and defenders prepare for the confrontation of Eteokles and Polyneices, with their riddling shield devices.

On the seven gods of Thebes and their attributes, and the meaning of seven in this play, see notes on the Chorus's entrance song (108-212) and on the central messenger scene (457-907).

The play has a Chorus of twelve (the traditional number for this period) and five speaking parts. There is some disagreement among manuscripts about the distribution of lines among Chorus and solo voices in the final lament. If the one we have followed is correct, the role of Ismene is limited to a few lines of lyric and can be assumed to have been played by an extra singer rather than by a full-fledged actor. In that case, *Seven Against Thebes* is a two-actor play—that is, all the speaking parts were distributed between two actors. On the other hand, if Ismene was played by an actor, it must be a three-actor play, since the text allows no time for an actor to leave the stage, change his mask and costume, and re-enter at 1281 as the Messenger of the magistrates of Thebes. This apparent economy in construction (two actors plus twelve members of the Chorus) is somewhat misleading. With the maximum of doubling (Theban citizens, at least twelve, become Theban soldiers; six Theban magistrates become six Theban champions; six armor-bearers become attendants of Antigone and Ismene) the play cannot be produced without twenty-four people on stage in addition to the actors and Chorus, and the smallest possible number of masks required (speaking and non-speaking parts together) is sixty-five.

NOTES ON THE TEXT

1 *children of Kadmos* The original city on the site of Thebes was called after Kadmos, the first settler (see Introduction II and Glossary). Perhaps as a reminder that the action takes place in a distant past, the play never speaks of Thebes or Thebans, only of the city of Kadmos, children of Kadmos, Kadmeians, etc.

2-3 *whoever has charge of affairs . . . holding the rudder* The metaphor of the ship of state, struggling in a stormy sea, a commonplace from Homer on, is the controlling image of *Seven Against Thebes*. Its treatment in this play is the most extended and developed in classical Greek literature. Nautical language is constantly used of the city and of the fighting men on both sides (e.g. 48-9, 87-9, 99, 248-52, 815, 965-79, 1014-16, 1265, 1379-81). The ship metaphor, which seems at first to apply entirely to the city, gradually comes to be associated with the house of Laios. The focus shifts from the ship of state, threatened by the storm of war, to the bark of death in which Eteokles and Polyneices are swept away by winds of wrath and surges of weeping (particularly 869-71 and 1087-1196). The gods of this storm are Ares and the Fury, the personifications of the violence and wrath of the house of Laios (Introduction II).

11-17 *And I, Eteokles, . . . so prove fitly named/for the city of the Kadmeians* This passage has hitherto been understood to say, "And I, Eteokles, would be multiplied in songs of mourning throughout the city. May

Zeus, Averter, forbid it and so prove fitly named for the city of Kadmeians." A minor change in the standard punctuation makes Eteokles rather than Zeus the one who is fitly named, and gives the first of many indications that his name may turn out to mean "truly bewept," rather than "justly famed" (Introduction v). The reference to weeping in Eteokles' name has gone undetected in modern times, hence the preference for the other punctuation.

97-8 On summoning the Curse and the Fury to defend the city, see Introduction III. The consequences of this act begin to appear in the central scene (819-20, 869, 878-9, 884-5, 895-6). The choral song that follows that scene (908-1009) gives the history of the joint operation of Curse and Fury in the house of Laios, and the final lament (1044-1280) celebrates the power of the Fury as the implementer of the Curse, saluting her in the same words as those with which Eteokles originally summons her, "Fury, whose power is great" (1245 and 1261).

108-212 Chorus's entrance song: the Chorus alternate between excited exclamation (108-39, and 181-200) and a formal prayer in which the seven gods are invoked first jointly (140-8), then individually (148-80), and again jointly (201-12). At 188, the Greek text names an eighth deity, Hera. Unlike the other gods named, she is given no attributes in the ode and has no function elsewhere in the play. These facts, combined with the thematic importance of the number seven in this choral song and in the design of the play, seem to us to justify the assumption that Hera does not belong in this prayer, but is there as the result of a copyist's misreading of one of Artemis' attributes, possibly *potnia theron*, "mistress of wild beasts." The Greek letters of this epithet could easily be mistaken for the reading of our MSS., *potnia Hera*, "Mistress Hera."

117 ai   Ai, E (1231), and Io (1234) are some of the many inarticulate cries of grief used in Greek tragedy.

120 *shields like staring eyes*   The Greek says "round white shields," a reference to the distinctive shape and color of the Argive shield, invented by the hero Proitos (see 459 with note). In the central messenger scene, the association of this round white shield with an eye that can cast an evil spell is repeatedly suggested.

137 *God of the Golden Helmet*   Perhaps Ares' helmet is connected with his role as apportioner of lots (see 920-5). For Ares as ancestral god see note on 164-72.

148-50 Zeus, king of the gods, is invoked first and alone as Accomplisher, and defender of Dike (Introduction II). His thunderbolt, several times invoked in the central scene, symbolizes his power to uphold Dike, the principle of order. The remaining six gods are invoked in pairs.

154-7 *Seven men . . . seven gates* The number seven is stressed again in this song at 200. It also structures the central scene. The seventh gate is the gate of destiny for Eteokles and Polyneices. The other gates have names, this one is simply called seventh, though in other versions of the story, it too had a name (note to 459). Apollo, who presides at the seventh gate, has the title *Hebdomagetes*, Lord of Sevens (1018-21). The structuring of the action by this number contributes to the sense of a fateful symmetry which brings the sons of Oedipus together. But for this purpose, another number might have served. The special significance of seven in this play seems to be its connection with Apollo, who, as god of harmony, musical (the seven-stringed lyre) and cosmic (the seven planets), presides over the ceremony of reconciliation and purification performed at the seventh gate.

158-63 Athena, armed with helmet, spear, and aegis, is a defender of civilization and order, Zeus' ally against the giants. (The aegis, symbol of Zeus' authority, is a goatskin worn in battle, either on her left arm as a shield or poncho-style as body armor, usually decorated with a gorgon mask; when shaken by Zeus, it makes a thunderstorm which creates panic in men.) She and Poseidon, inventor of the bridle which tames horses, and the ship which masters the waves, are coupled here (as in their joint cult in Athens) as expressions of the controlled force that overcomes the kind of mindless violence (storm of Ares and the Fury, brute animal rage) which threatens to engulf the city (see notes on 530 and 557).

164-72 Ares and Aphrodite are the ancestral gods of the city, parents of Harmonia, the wife of Kadmos. The ambiguity of the relationships among the members of the house of Laios, linked to each other by the unbreakable ties of blood, but also enemies to the death, is expressed in the treatment of Ares, who is not only invoked as an ancestor and protector (see also 134-9, 509) but also imagined as inspiring the attackers (63, 74, 88, 152, 612). Like Oedipus and his sons, he is both outsider and insider, friend as an ancestral god; stranger because of his links with the alien world of Thrace. At 311-12, and 421-4, he

seems to be neither friend nor stranger but simply the spirit of violence. Aphrodite is not named elsewhere in the play, but her force
is felt in the perverted blood-lust of 866-8, 874-7, and in the many
passages which more or less explicitly suggest incestuous desire as
the cause of the hostility among the males in the house of Laios (see
particularly 559-64, 719-32, 951-64, 1086, 1118-29, 1170-6, 1279-80).

173-80 Apollo, wolf-slayer, and his sister Artemis with her arrows, are both invoked
as hunters, that is, curbers of the wild animal force that threatens
the city; also as purifiers, since it is with their arrows that Artemis
and Apollo both inflict sickness and restore health.

204 *strangely spoken* Aeschylus uses an adjective that means "speaking differ-
ently." The most natural explanation is that he is referring to the
fact that the attackers, with the exception of Polyneices, are not
Thebans, and therefore speak different dialects of Greek. Their alien
speech makes them more menacing. Some think "strangely spoken"
means that the attackers actually speak a foreign language. These are
the critics who read the play as a commentary on the Persian Wars,
in which the attackers represent impious barbarism, the defenders
rational and restrained Hellenism. Such an interpretation restricts
the reference of the play by ignoring many aspects of the imagery. It
also has to explain away the fact that Aeschylus twice uses the adjective "Achaian" in connection with the attackers (44, 403). At 403
we have translated "Achaian" with "Hellene."

232 *man, woman, any who joins with such a one* The Greek, which as it stands
means, "man and woman and whatever is in between," is not intelligible. We have therefore assumed a corruption and substituted a
plausible conjecture.

234-6 *the pebble . . . the people's decree* Judges, casting their votes for acquittal
or conviction, sometimes used pebbles as ballots. The penalty for
treason was to be stoned to death. The pebbles which convicted a
man of treason are here assimilated to the stones with which the
sentence was executed. Perhaps the storm of stones hurled at the
towers of Thebes (255-6 and 376-7) should be connected with this
passage.

273-6 Eteokles offers the Chorus a bit of popular wisdom in the form of a riddle
whose full implications he seems not to understand. Like Laios and
Oedipus before him, he hopes to save the city and be the author of

well-being for himself and others; but, also like Laios and Oedipus, he is a defier of authority (Introduction II, III, IV). Perhaps there is a play on the notion of mother/wife. Eteokles would like to be at once the child (Well-Being) and the husband (Him-Who-Saves).

283-8 Eteokles is referring to the pre-battle ritual of taking the omens (see 460-2). However, the women are not usurping this masculine role. The supplication of the gods of the city in time of crisis is a traditional function of women. Compare the supplication of Athena by the women of Troy (*Iliad*, VI. 286-310).

338-9 Apollo's chant is the paean—a song of victory, but also of healing and purification. The Greek does not name Apollo but uses a verb that means, "to sing a paean" (see 790, 1046, 1111, 1208-13).

346 *Dirke . . . Ismenos* In the dry climate of Greece, where water quite visibly brings life, to invoke the local springs and rivers is to draw attention to the life-giving, that is, parental aspect of the land.

388 *Ocean's daughters* In the Greek text, they are called Tethys' daughters. Springs and rivers are the daughters of Okeanos and his consort Tethys. We have substituted the parent more likely to be recognized by a modern audience.

414-17 Part of the marriage ceremony was the procession of singing boys and girls which escorted the bride from her father's house to her husband's house. The sack of the city is imagined as an inverted marriage ritual whose consummation is rape and death (446-51).

457-907 Central messenger scene: The scene has two sections. In the first, which ends at 848, the Scout describes the attacking champions, with their shields, and for each of these Eteokles selects and dispatches to the walls a suitable opponent. The climax of this section is Eteokles' decision to defend the seventh gate in person. The climax of the whole scene is the revelation of the device on Eteokles' shield. This is postponed until near the end of the second section. It is gradually built up to as Eteokles assumes his armor piece by piece and the Chorus tries to dissuade him from his decision to go to the seventh gate. Both the descriptions of the shields and the arming of the hero are conventions of the epic which Aeschylus has converted to dramatic purposes. See the shields of Agamemnon and Achilles (*Iliad* XIX.32-40, XVIII.478-608) and the arming of Paris and Agamemnon (*Iliad*

III.330-8, XIX.16-45). As in the epic, the emblems on the shields provide an opportunity for enlarging and deepening the meaning of the action. Shield devices were traditionally a kind of magic designed to terrify the enemy and make the bearer invincible—"engines" (*exeuremata*, 811) of war against which appropriate counter-measures must be taken. Compare the song that Eteokles orders the Chorus to sing, "giving confidence to friends,/ letting loose fear to the enemy" (342-3). Each of the first five emblems of the attackers is designed to unman the Thebans by an allusion to the potentially disastrous problems of the house of Laios. The first and last are the most overt —the moon, with her reminder of Oedipus' fatal meeting with his father (note to 473), and the Sphinx, symbol of Oedipus' and Thebes's failure to understand their true identity. The other three express, in ascending order of violence, the defiance of Dike which undid Laios and all who associated with him (Introduction II and IV). The language leaves it uncertain as to whether the defenders named by Eteokles are actually on stage, and, with one exception, we are not told what devices they have on their shields. But that exception is instructive. Hyperbios, confronting Hippomedon who has Typhon on his shield, has as his device the slayer of Typhon, thunder-wielding Zeus (629-39), one of the seven gods whose images stand on the stage (148-80). In this case, anyway, Eteokles pits device against device. Furthermore, we must imagine that when Eteokles takes shield in hand (895) he displays a suitable device, even though the text does not allude to it directly. For not only is the blank shield reserved for Amphiaraos (735-41); Polyneices' shield device is carefully described and strongly emphasized. Since the brothers are counterparts of each other in every way, Eteokles' shield must have an answering device. And the Fury is the proper counterpart of Dike (cf. note to 895-6). In two cases, then, the shield device is a significant part of the defender's equipment. It seems likely therefore that the devices of the other defenders were not overlooked. Since these devices are not mentioned they can only have been presented visually, by the defenders themselves present on the stage with their shields. Dramatically too it is more satisfying if, as in the case of Polyneices, the description of each attacker is answered not simply by another description but also by an actual champion with an answering shield device. Hyperbios' device provides the clue to what the devices of the remaining five might be. For each attacker one of the seven gods to whose statues the Chorus pray and make offerings in their opening song is as appropriate an opponent as Zeus is for Hippomedon. If each defender has on his shield one of these gods, Eteokles' prayer (336), "May the gods strengthen our men and direct our spears," is, in the most literal sense, enacted. As the time approaches for Eteokles to reveal his shield device, the presence of the image of Aphrodite, the only one of the seven gods not yet assigned to a shield, increases the irony and suspense. Symmetry would make her Eteokles' device, and the Chorus speak of lust (868) and desire (874). But Aphrodite remains unassigned. For the emblem of love and creation Eteokles substitutes the Fury (note to 895-6), the emblem of hatred and death—confirmation that, like Laios and Oedipus, he too can father only destruction. The Curse is still at work. The assignment of gods to shields, dictated by the attributes of the gods and the character of the warriors, as well as the device which each confronts, results in a meaningful symmetry: Ares, Athena, Poseidon, Zeus, Artemis, Apollo, Fury, with Zeus, the giver of Dike, in the center, Ares and the Fury, the implementers of the storm, framing the group, and the two pairs Athena/Poseidon and Artemis/Apollo in between.

459 *the gate of Proitos*   On Proitos see note to 120. By naming the gate of Proitos first and repeating the name at the end of the speech (484) Aeschylus draws attention at the beginning of the scene to the roundness and whiteness, the resemblance to eyes that can cast evil spells, of the shields of the attackers. In addition, Tydeus' device, the moon, is actually referred to as "the eye of night" (475). The names and locations of the gates of Thebes were established by tradition, though there are minor variations from author to author. Aeschylus gives the seven gates with the captains attacking and defending them as follows:

1. *Proitides* (gate of Proitos)—Tydeus, Melanippos.
2. *Elektrai* (gate of Elektra)—Kapaneus, Polyphontes.
3. *Neïstai* (gate of Neïs)—Eteoklos, Megareus.
4. *Onkaiai* (gate of Athena Onka)—Hippomedon, Hyperbios.
5. *Borrhaiai* (Northern gate)—Parthenopaios, Aktor.
6. *Homoloides* (Homoloian gate)—Amphiaraos, Lasthenes.
7. Seventh gate, not given a name by Aeschylus, though elsewhere called *Hypsistai* or *Kreneiai*—Polyneices, Eteokles.

The order is dramatic not geographical. The geographical order, proceeding clockwise from the northernmost point of the citadel, is

> Borrhaiai (5), Proitides (1), Homoloides (6), Elektrai (2), On-kaiai (4), the seventh gate (7), Neïstai (3).

461 *Ismenos* To cross the stream with an armed force would signal the opening of hostilities. The gods oppose this as sacrilege.

473 *the triple goddess of the three ways* This epithet is not in the Greek text. We have added it to make the allusion to Hekate more explicit. Hekate ("Diana of the Crossways") presides over the fork in the road, the place of fateful choice. For Aeschylus' audience the allusion to the moon would have been sufficient to suggest Hekate and the place "where three ways meet" (Introduction IV). Both Hekate and the moon express the enigmatic, changeable (threefold) nature of woman, and are closely associated in myth and cult with each other and with the Fury (Introduction II).

508 *seed of the dragon's teeth* Here and at 583, Aeschylus calls attention to the strife-torn origins of Thebans (Introduction II)—another hint that the springs of violence are inside as well as outside the city. To Tydeus, who expresses nothing but battle lust, the Ares on Melanippos' shield is a suitable answer, and his concentrated maleness is directed against the moon/Hekate, the embodiment of all female power, creative and destructive.

512 For Dike, see Introduction II and IV and Glossary.

530 *giant-slaying lightnings* This phrase renders the single Greek word *eris* (strife). According to a very probable suggestion, Aeschylus is here following Hesiod (*Theogony* 709-10), who used this word of the lightning which was Zeus' weapon in the war between the gods and giants. The Scout compares Kapaneus to one of these giants (523), and his emblem, a naked man with a flaming torch, recalls their primitive methods of warfare. In the battle with the gods, they relied on brute strength and such weapons as nature offered—enormous rocks, and torches made from trees.

557 The warrior Athena, who helped Zeus quell the giants, is frequently represented in the act of piercing a fallen giant with her spear (note on 158-63). She is the natural antagonist for giant-like Kapaneus and his shield device.

581 *and a certain, apt fortune goes with him* Both Eteoklos, with his maddened horses, and the man on his shield hurl themselves against the walls of the city like a tidal wave. It is "apt fortune," therefore, that Poseidon, bridler of horses and tamer of the waves, is arrayed against them on the shield of Megareus. The description of Megareus standing firm in the storm of war (584-6) suggests Poseidon calming the storm.

598 The gate is named for the shrine of Athena Onka (a local cult name of unclear significance) which stood just outside the gate. Cf. the shrine of Artemis outside the gate of Elektra (555-6) and the tomb of Amphion outside the Northern gate (648).

601 *the enormous threshing-floor* This image alludes both to the roundness of the shield, since the Greek threshing-floor is circular, and to the fecundity of violence—a pervasive theme. See particularly 749-50.

625 Hermes is, among many other things, a god of luck or fortunate coincidence.

628 Typhon, earthborn like the giants, was more monstrous and more powerful than they. (See Glossary.) Hippomedon seems to share some of the monstrous quality of his shield device.

658-76 There is a fairly general feeling among editors that the line-order of this passage as it appears in the MSS. is not correct. We have profited from their arguments by producing a new line-order, which seems to us to give the speech a more coherent structure than do any of their suggestions.

661 The Sphinx (see Glossary) is another type of the mysterious threefold female goddess (cf. note to 473). Like her, Parthenopaios is an enigmatic combination of opposing qualities—resembling both a beautiful girl and a beast of prey. The threat of the Sphinx is answered by Artemis who also expresses woman's multiple enigmatic nature. As mistress of wild beasts and huntress, she is both the patron of Parthenopaios, the wild animal of the Arcadian mountains, and the one who will hunt him down (Introduction iv).

714-16 On the meaning of Polyneices' name see Introduction v.

734 *"The fate I expect is not without honor"* Amphiaraos knew the expedition against Thebes was impious and doomed, but was tricked into join-

ing it. As a reward for his uprightness he was spared death in battle, the fate of the other Argive leaders. During the fighting Zeus caused the earth to open and swallow him up with his chariot and horses. (See Introduction IV.)

754 *When men lose their humanity* This expresses the pejorative meaning of the adjective *echthroxenos* (literally, "hating strangers," i.e., violating the laws of hospitality). At 770, Eteokles applies the same adjective as a term of praise to Lasthenes, "who hates outsiders." This is one of the many instances where Aeschylus exploits the ambiguities of language to point up the fundamental similarity of attackers and defenders.

769-75 The blank shield of Amphiaraos expresses the refusal of all disguises, the commitment to truth of a seer and priest of Apollo, the god of truth and prophecy. In sending out Lasthenes, with Apollo on his shield, against him, Eteokles pits truth against truth, just as in confronting the Sphinx with Artemis he pits female enigma against female enigma.

805 Dike (see Introduction II and IV) now appears in visible form. Eteokles, in the first speech of this scene, has claimed her as an ally and blood-relative of the Thebans (512-13). Amphiaraos has denied that she can sanction violence against parents (722-32).

808 *"I shall bring this man to his harbor"* Aeschylus uses the same verb (*katagein*) here and at 827. It means both "to lead down into Hades" and "to bring to shore." The shore which both brothers ultimately reach is in fact the shore of Hades (1087-98).

816-48 Eteokles confronts a triple enigma—his own name, his brother's name, and the name of Dike. He first links his name with weeping and then tries to deny the connection (Introduction V). He then reiterates Amphiaraos' interpretation of Polyneices' name (714-16), and finally decides to test in action whether Dike is fitly named.

847 *Quickly, bring my armor* In the Greek text, Eteokles calls not for his armor but for his greaves. In the arming scenes of Greek literature (note to 457-907) the greaves are the first item that the hero puts on. To call for one's greaves is therefore the signal to begin arming. The order in which the other pieces of armor are assumed is also, with one

minor variation, fixed—breastplate, sword, helmet, shield, spear. In contrast to the relatively small hoplite shield carried by Eteokles (he refers to himself as *hoplites*, "man in full armor," 905), which was simply secured by two grips to the left arm and hand, the "man-covering shield" of Homeric epic was put on *before* the helmet, since it was anchored to the body by a strap that went over the head.

861-907 On Eteokles' preoccupation with fame in this passage, see Introduction v.

873 *Phoibos*   The use of this epithet of Apollo, which means "the shining one," suggests that the race of Laios are not fit to see the light of day. Compare the description of their ultimate fate in 1087-98.

885 *when the gods accept a sacrifice at your hands*   The gods accept sacrifice only from ritually clean hands. The Chorus try to persuade Eteokles that purification is still possible since he has not yet shed kindred blood.

895-6 Eteokles' shield device must answer the shield device of Polyneices with a comparable and related force. The proper counterpart to Dike is her implementer the Fury, whose renewed onslaught Eteokles acknowledges as he takes his shield in hand. Since the Fury and Dike are two aspects of one cosmic order, their confrontation expresses a deadlock which only the death of both brothers can resolve.

896-7 *They were . . . omens that came in dreams*   This must refer to a prophetic dream in one of the earlier plays of the trilogy, whose real meaning only now becomes clear to Eteokles. Compare the dreams of Atossa in *Persians* and Clytemnestra in *Libation Bearers*.

898 *split by an iron sword*   Iron, which was imported from the region north of the Black Sea (Scythia, Chalybia), and Ares, who is associated with the neighboring region of Thrace, become identified in the following song, and are used interchangeably throughout the rest of the play to represent the just divider and apportioner of the inheritance (920-6 and 1039-40, 1129, 1150-8, 1191-6). In this scene, Eteokles is turned into iron ("man in full armor"), the remorseless instrument of justice. He becomes the embodiment of Ares.

946 *the midmost Pythian navel*   Apollo's shrine at Delphi, reputed to be the navel of earth. Woman is the ultimate source of this enigmatic pronouncement, as she is of the other enigmas that confront the race of Laios.

967-9 The threefold wave alludes, among other things, to the three generations of the house of Laios (Introduction IV).

1009 *the fleet-footed Fury*   Like her inability to weep or sleep, the Fury's swiftness of foot is proverbial. The transgressor cannot move her to pity, or hide from her all-seeing eye, or run fast enough to escape her overtaking stride.

1018 *Apollo, the holy Lord of Sevens*   See note on 154-7.

1022-43 That the line-order of this passage (803-21 of the Greek text) is not correct in our MSS. is clear from the fact that line 1030 of our version occurs twice—as line 804 of the Greek text, the second line of the passage, and again as line 820, the next to the last line of the passage. In the MSS., the passage ends, "The city is safe, but the two kings of one blood/ have spilled their shared stream out, earth has drunk up/ the blood of their mutual slaughter" (820-1 of the Greek text). The repeated line is connected by sense and syntax with the line that follows it at the end of the passage, but not in any necessary way with the line that precedes it there. It makes nonsense of the sequence of thought at the beginning of the passage. Editors have called either for drastic rearrangement of the line-order of the whole passage, combined with elimination of one occurrence of the repeated line, or for elimination of various blocks of lines, including one or both occurrences of the repeated line, on the assumption that the repetition is the result of the conflation of the original text with the work of a fourth-century interpolator. Our solution is simpler. It removes only one line, and transposes only two. If the repeated line is removed from the beginning where it clearly does not belong, the pattern of the exchange between Chorus and Scout becomes clear. By their questions and exclamations, the Chorus, who guess what has happened, finally induce the Scout to announce the news that both they and he find almost too horrible to put into words. This information, contained in the lines quoted above, belongs not at the end of the passage, after the news it conveys has already been commented on, but where we have put it, after the Chorus's last demand, "Go on; speak your heavy things."

1044-1280 The lament: Some, but not all, of the editors who regard the final scene as an interpolation consider the participation of Antigone and Ismene in the lament and the lines that the Chorus address to them

(1099-1117) as part of the interpolation (see note on 1099-1117 and Introduction III).

1046-50 The Chorus build into the lament a victory song of Hades, Ate, and the Curses (1111, 1208-16). Since the city has been, at least temporarily, delivered by the triumph of these forces, to lament the deaths of Eteokles and Polyneices is to celebrate the victory of the city.

1060 *like a Maenad* The followers of Dionysos improvise songs and dances in a state of ecstatic possession by the god of life and creativity. But the Chorus's ecstatic song celebrates death not life (compare 612-13). The victory song which is also a lament (see note to 1046-50) involves a similar inversion.

1087-98 Another ritual is alluded to here, and inverted. The language that describes the ship suggests the sacred ship of Apollo that the Athenians annually sent to the island of Delos on the anniversary of Theseus' victory over the Minotaur—a victory which saved seven youths and seven maidens from being sacrificed to the monster. The sacred ship went to Delos (the name means "clearly visible"), Apollo's shore, in commemoration of a rescue; the "black-sailed ship of grief" goes to the "unseen" shore, "untrodden by Apollo." For the transfer of ship imagery from the city to the house of Laios, see note to 2-3.

1099-1117 Editors who regard the participation of Antigone and Ismene in the lament as the work of an interpolator bracket these lines, and give the lines attributed to Antigone and Ismene to semi-choruses.

1113 *the menstrual pulse* The Greek text refers not to menstruation, but to a piece of female dress with which a modern audience is not familiar —the band which restrained the breasts. The purpose of the allusion is to emphasize the common femininity of the Chorus and Antigone and Ismene—their sisterhood in grief.

1334-5 *drag him . . . folds of my cloak* We read this passage as a reference to the tradition that Antigone dragged the body of Polyneices in her robe to Eteokles' funeral pyre. Pausanias (IX.25,2) refers to a monument that marked the place of "Antigone's dragging." The Greek is ambiguous. According to some, what Antigone carries in the folds of her robe is earth to sprinkle on the corpse of Polyneices, so that he will have token burial. This is the version that Sophocles follows (or invented?) in *Antigone*.

1352-3 *Last of the gods . . . the last word* In the MSS., where these words (one line in the Greek) follow 1349, the sequence of thought from 1349 to the end of the passage is, as many editors have noted, somewhat jumbled. If they are moved to the end of the passage, where we have put them, they provide a fitting commentary on the whole episode, and the three preceding lines follow naturally one from the other.

GLOSSARY

ADRASTOS, king of Argos and commander-in-chief of the Argive army. The only Argive leader not killed in the attack on Thebes.

AKTOR, son of Oinops; Theban captain at the Northern gate.

AMPHIARAOS, son of Oikles; priest of Apollo, Argive captain at the Homoloian gate.

AMPHION, a Theban hero, who caused the walls of Thebes to rise by playing on his lyre. His grave was near the Northern gate.

ANTIGONE, daughter of Oedipus.

ARES, god of war and the personification of strife; father by Aphrodite of Harmonia (q.v.)

ATE, personification of folly; a kind of blindness or insanity that makes men act in defiance of moral law.

CURSES, the personified prayers for justice of those whose rights have been violated. They are implemented by the Fury.

DIKE, the personification of the fundamental principle of right and order.

DIRKE, one of the springs of Thebes.

ENYO, goddess of war-like frenzy.

ETEOKLES, son of Oedipus; Theban captain at the seventh gate.

ETEOKLOS, Argive captain at the gate of Neïs.

FURY (Erinys), the personification of the wrath which pursues the violators of Dike, of which she is, in her other aspect, the maternal cherisher and fosterer.

HARMONIA, daughter of Ares and Aphrodite; wife of Kadmos.

HIPPOMEDON, Argive captain at the gate of Athena.

HYPERBIOS, son of Oinops; Theban captain at the gate off Athena.

ISMENE, daughter of Oedipus.
ISMENOS, one of the streams of Thebes.

KADMOS, the legendary founder of Thebes, son of Agenor, king of Tyre. With his wife Harmonia he is the progenitor of the royal house of Thebes.
KAPANEUS, Argive captain at the gate of Elektra.

LAIOS, father of Oedipus.
LASTHENES, Theban captain at the Homoloian gate.

MAENAD, frenzied woman worshiper of Dionysos.
MEGAREUS, son of Kreon, descended from one of the heroes that sprang from the dragon's teeth sown by Kadmos; Theban captain at the gate of Neïs.
MELANIPPOS, Theban captain at the gate of Proitos; descended from one of the heroes who sprang from the dragon's teeth sown by Kadmos.

OEDIPUS, son of Laios, father of Eteokles, Polyneices, Antigone, Ismene.

PARTHENOPAIOS, an Arcadian, son of Atalanta; Argive captain at the Northern gate.
PHOBOS, personified divinity of fear or battle terror.
PHOIBOS, epithet of Apollo.
POLYNEICES, son of Oedipus; Argive captain at the seventh gate.
POLYPHONTES, Theban captain at the gate of Elektra.

SPARTOI, "sown men," the ancestors of the Thebans. They sprang from the soil where Kadmos sowed the dragon's teeth.
SPHINX, threefold demon with the head of a beautiful woman, the body of a lion, and the wings of a bird; she killed those who could not answer her riddle.

TEIRESIAS, blind Theban gifted with prophecy.
TYDEUS, Argive captain at the gate of Proitos.
TYPHON, a monster with a hundred snake-heads, fiery eyes, and a tremendous voice; was vanquished by Zeus with his thunder and lightning in a duel that shook the universe.